Out of Babylon

Up to Jerusalem

**Challenging Centuries of Misinterpretation
of the Virgin Birth Theology**

Vicki Wolfe

Copyright © 2015
Out of Babylon Up to Jerusalem
Vicki Wolfe

ISBN: 978-0692950258

Printed by CreateSpace

Cover Design by Vicki Wolfe

Dedication

This book is dedicated to all those in pursuit of God's Torah (Gods word, wisdom, instruction).
This book could not have been written were it not for the vast controversial opinions of disharmony within the body of believers that has brought this book from a burden in my heart to its publication.

Contents

Chapter One

The Forbidden Fruit

If one were to inquire of most people as to what the specific fruit was of the tree of knowledge of good and evil in the Garden of Eden, a large consensus would resoundingly state, an apple.
You may even be told that everyone knows that, while receiving a look as though you had been hiding under a rock all your life.

As children most of us subtly learned from our Sunday school days that the forbidden fruit was an apple. As our teacher told the children's version of the story of the Garden of Eden, we were busily coloring an apple with our crayons. Our teacher may or may not have ever actually stated that the forbidden fruit was an apple, but as children we certainly knew how to connect the dots, coloring book page and story, equate.

One may be surprised to learn that nowhere in the entire Bible does it state, or even hint at, that the forbidden fruit was that of an apple. Yet, down through the ages humans have assumed and readily accepted it to be just that, an apple.

What if someone came along and said to you that the forbidden fruit was not an apple, but rather it was a fig and that this premise could be Biblically authenticated? Most likely you would be quite skeptical, so let's examine Scripture to see if there is any telling clue.

[1] *Genesis 3:6-7*

> *And the woman perceived that the tree was good for eating and that it was a delight to the eyes, and that the tree was desirable as a means of wisdom, and she took of its fruit and ate; and she gave also to her husband with her, and he ate.*
> *Then the eyes of both of them were opened and they realized that they were naked; and they sewed fig leaves together and made themselves loin covering.*

With careful examination of the above two verses, we see a subtle clue in the text that would indicate what the actual forbidden fruit was. Adam and Eve's actions were a continuous uninterrupted sequence of events that unfolded in a short span of time:

Eve saw the fruit, ate the fruit, and gave the fruit to Adam who was with her, Adam ate the fruit, both their eyes were opened, both realized they were naked and they sewed Fig Leaves together to cover themselves.

---

1 Scriptures unmarked without initials is this book author's own translation. All other Scriptures are marked accordingly to there collective translations.

Neither Adam nor Eve had moved from their location, they were standing next to a fig tree from the moment they ate the fruit to the moment they covered themselves with fig leaves.

The text certainly gives a strong indication that it was a fig, but is this hinting at something enough evidence to support the premise as absolute? I believe it does, however, in a later chapter of this book we will see additional proof positive that the forbidden fruit was indeed a fig, but for now this will have to suffice, as many subjects need to be addressed before the epilogue.

The Orchard

The Bible is likened to a beautiful orchard/garden, it has many layers within layers, yielding vast and plentiful satisfying spiritual food for us to partake in. The Hebrew word for Orchard is Pardes; the acronym is PRDS with each letter representing a unique way of seeing the depth and beauty of Gods garden (Bible).

P - P'shat: its literal meaning is "simple," the plain literal sense of the text.

R - Remez: its literal meaning is "hinting," the text is hinting at something not readily seen in the plain text. Like connecting the dots if you will.

D - Drash/ Midrash:
its literal meaning is "search," allegorical, like a parable.

S - Sod: its literal meaning is "secret," as in obscure not readily seen.

Through this method we are literally examining and partaking in God's PaRDeS (orchard/garden) that He created and placed humankind in to be nurtured, partaking of the Tree of Life that God ordained[2], it is through God's Torah/Word[3] that sets the standard to measure all things.

Various aspects of the Newest Testament have been misunderstood and misinterpreted throughout the ages, that in fact many Newest Testament Scriptures actually say the very opposite of what traditional Christianity claims it to say. This is due mainly in part of traditional Christianity's lack of knowledge and understanding of the Oldest Testament and its Hebraic content.

An obvious directive for believers in Messiah Yeshua (Christ Jesus) comes from the Newest Testament Scriptures that point believers to the Oldest Testament Scriptures, can be found in the book of Acts.

Acts 17:11

> *Now these (people) were of nobler character than those in Thessalonica, they eagerly received the word and everyday examined the Scriptures (Oldest Testament[4]) to see if the things (Paul/Sha'ul was saying) were true.*

---

2 Genesis 2:16-17

3 Proverbs 3:18 "she and her" refer to: Gods Torah (Gods word, wisdom, instruction). e.g. Gods word is a tree of life to those who grasp its wisdom, whoever holds fast to its wisdom, will be made happy. "Torah - תורה - Gods word, wisdom, instruction." The commonly accepted English word "law" gives a wrong impression.

4 The Newest Testament had not been written as of yet, it was in the making, therefore, the only Scriptures they could have examined were that of the Oldest Testament.

These people of Berea studied the Oldest Testament, for they, having wisdom and understanding, knew that the Oldest Testament is in fact God's message to the world, the standard in which to measure all things.

Furthermore,

Proverbs 18:17 states:
   The first to state his case seems right, till the other one comes and cross-examines.

Accordingly, this is exactly what those of noble character did; they cross-examined Paul by checking the Oldest Testament to see if what Paul had been teaching them were in fact true.

This is what this book is about, cross-examination, in holding traditional belief systems up to Scripture to see if traditional beliefs will stand or fall. To bring back the hearts of the people to the one true God, the God of Abraham (Avraham), Isaac (Yitz'chak) and Jacob (Ya'akov), the God of Israel.

Presenting an accurate picture of God's anointed one, the Messiah[5]. One must not present a different Messiah than the one God has established as the Messiah, as set forth in the Oldest Testament[6]. Otherwise, one will attach themselves to

---

5 The English title "Messiah" comes directly from the Hebrew word "מָשִׁיחַ - Mashiach," whereas the English title "Christ" comes through the Greek word "Χριστου - Christos." The literal meaning of the Hebrew word "Mashiach" means " the anointed one" here in context, "the anointed one of God."

6 The commonly used English title "Old Testament," better said "Oldest Testament" is known in the Hebrew language as the "Tanakh - תנ״ך - TNK" an acronym representing the three parts of the Oldest Testament: **T** - Torah (Teaching / instruction), **N** – Nevi'im (Prophets), and **K** - Ketuvim (Writings).

false Messiah's, specifically the anti-Messiah, and its false doctrines therein.

It is God's Word, His Torah (wisdom, instruction) that sets the standard to measure all things.

Out of Babylon

Revelation 17:5

> *On her forehead a name written: Mystery Babylon the great, mother of whores and of the earth's depravity.*

A great deal of pagan mythology is rooted in ancient Babylon, it having influenced the world throughout the ages with its perversions.

In its day, ancient Babylon was the emporium of the known world and was considered: "the mistress of the world." Although the physical location of Babylon no longer exists, its spiritual condition has spanned the ages right into our modern day.

Babylon, the mother, is none other than the mistress of the world, the whores being her children, and great, is their rebellion and the earth's depravity. Both bewitching humankind with their deadly charms and lies, the world fascinated with its mysticism, drunk with power and luxuries, bloated with arrogance!

In the Bible, Babylon epitomizes evil, that of a worldly view system with its false teachings, that which ensnares. Whereas Jerusalem exemplifies righteousness, adhering to God's word and His ways. *(Isaiah. 2:3, Micah. 4:2)*

The flood being a reset for humanity, it wasn't long, in fact, it was a mere few generations after the flood that we find the first rebellion against God, the Creator and Sustainer of life. Talk about a self inflicted wound.

Flavius Josephus, a first century historian, gives insight to the founder of Babylon, in reference to Scripture of *Genesis 10:8-10; 11:1-9*, he writes the following[7]:

Antiquities of the Jews – Book 1:113-117
Now it was Nimrod who excited them to such an affront and contempt of God. He was the grandson of Ham, the son of Noah, a bold man, and of great strength of hand. He persuaded them not to ascribe it to God as if it was through his means they were happy, but to believe that it was their own courage which procured that happiness.

He also gradually changed the government into tyranny, seeing no other way of turning men from the fear of God, but to bring them into a constant dependence upon his power. He also said he would be revenged on God, if he should have a mind to drown the world again; for that he would build a tower too high for the waters to be able to reach! And that he would avenge himself on God for destroying their forefathers!

Now the multitude were very ready to follow the determination of Nimrod, and to esteem it a piece of cowardice to submit to God: and they built a tower, neither sparing any pains nor being in any degree negligent about the work: and, by reason of the multitude of hands employed in it it grew very high sooner than anyone could expect;

But the thickness of it was so great, and it was so strongly built, that thereby its great height seemed, upon the view, to be less than it really was. It was built of burnt brick cemented together with mortar, made of bitumen, that it might not be liable to admit water. When God saw that they acted so madly he did not resolve to destroy

---

7   The Works of Josephus, translated by William Whiston. Tenth printing - January 1995, Copyright 1987 by Hendrickson Publisher, Inc.

them utterly, since they were not growing wiser by the destruction of the former sinners;
But he caused tumult among them, by producing in them divers languages: and causing that, through the multitude of those language, they should not be able to understand one another. The place wherein they built the tower is now called Babylon; because of the confusion of that language which they readily understood before; for the Hebrews mean by the word Babel, Confusion.

Genesis 10:9 ½ reads:
He (Nimrod) was a mighty hunter before HASHEM[8]

In context; "mighty hunter" as signifying "a man of chase," here "in pursuit of ungodliness" "Before the LORD" or "in the face of the LORD," as signifying "in opposition to the LORD."
Nimrod is the archetype of rebellion against the Almighty. Nimrod and his followers, lacking sense and humility, this is why Josephus states: "they acted so madly."

> Humankind rears his own tyrant leaders, idols,
> lies and perversions; he toils in preparation for
> his own calamity, is he insane?

Nonetheless, these senseless people were in dire need of God's mercy in restraining their hand from the direction they were headed. Since these people had not grown wiser from the destruction of the former sinners, God in His mercy, by confusing their language, afforded them the opportunity to reconsider their sinful ways.

---

8 HASHEM - literally THE NAME: "יהוה - YHVH" the ineffable name of God. HASHEM: lit. "THE NAME," refers to The LORD, the God of Israel. English Bibles written as: THE LORD, or Jehovah, or ADONAI, or HASHEM. ADONAI, refers to The LORD, the God of Israel. In modern era, it is uncertain as to how to pronounce the Name of God "יהוה - YHVH."

The word Babylon derives its name from the word Babel, literally translated means "confuse or confusion." Nimrod and followers were certainly confused in the scheme of things, so to confuse their language was quite befitting them, "Poetic Justice," yet, "Merciful."

The physical location of the ancient city of Babylon would be in the region of what is now modern day Iraq. However, our focus is not set on a specific physical place per se, but rather our focus is more on a specific frame of mind, as can be seen from the following Scripture.

Revelation 14:8
> *Also another, a second angel followed, saying:*
> *Fallen, Fallen is Babylon the great, who out of it made all the nations drink the wine of wrath of her fornication/Idolatry.*

Today, as well as in the first century when the book of Revelation was written, in both eras the physical location of Babylon being nonexistent[9].
The question then begging for an answer, why does Scripture state Babylon's future: as being destroyed at the end of the last age, when in fact the physical location of Babylon is nonexistent?
Will Babylon's physical location rise again, or does Babylon represent a worldwide frame of mind of its spiritual condition in depravity?

---

9 By 141 B.C.E. (Before Common Era) with the rise of the Parthian Empire in control of the region, Babylon was in complete desolation and obscurity.

Consider the following Scriptures:

Jeremiah 51:12-13

> *Raise the banner against the walls of Babylon; strengthen the watch, rouse the guards, prepare the ambush, for HASHEM has planned and will carry out what He had spoken concerning the inhabitants of Babylon.*
>
> *You who dwell by many waters, abundant treasures, your end has come and the measure of your brutality.*

The above verses refer to Babylon's physical location of that being destroyed and no longer inhabited. It is in the past tense, as Babylon is in complete desolation and obscurity physically.

Keeping in mind a previous verse; *Revelation 14:8*

"Babylon has fallen" with regard to:

Revelation 17:1-2

> *Then came one of the seven angels that had the seven bowls, and he said to me, come, I will show you the judgment of the great harlot who sits by many waters, with whom the kings of the earth committed fornication/idolatry, and they that dwell on the earth have become drunk from the wine of her whoring.*

The above verses refer to Babylon's spiritual condition, that of vast depravity. It is in the perfect future tense, expressing the certainty of its judgment.

Another way of saying "the great harlot who sits by many waters" is; "Babylon's teachings are worldwide, as many waters refer to many peoples, many nations/ kingdoms."

Whoredom (idolatry) may very well have started at the physical locale of ancient Babylon, of which, literally did sit by many waters. Ancient Babylon sat between the Tigris and Euphrates Rivers, of which had numerous waterways throughout its entire city, along with the populace world. However, all land mass on earth, all seven continents literally "sit by many waters," along with its populace. All inhabitants of earth have been exposed to the lies that came out of ancient Babylon. Therefore, those having embraced its false doctrine, those inhabitants having the same mindset, therein dwell within the realm of Babylon.

Ancient Babylon being the great whore, nations and or individuals of the earth have committed fornication with her, by embracing its false teachings, some more so than others. Each spreading the contagious disease like a plague, it moves forward, person to person, country to country and from generation to generation. So too goes every whim of doctrine in our modern age of technology, only today it moves as fast as the speed of light.

Although its false teachings are worldwide, it is not to say that every individual person has embraced it.

> "It is not the knowledge of evil, but the
> succumbing to it, which is deadly; man may
> see the forbidden fruit, he need not eat of it.
> Man himself can make or mar his destiny."[10]

The false teachings of ancient Babylon have certainly darkened the world throughout the ages, concealing the light

---

10 The Pentateuch and Haftorahs, edited by Dr. J.H. Hertz, C.H. late Chief Rabbi of the British Empire. second edition 1981 page 197

of truth. However, Yeshua (Jesus[11]), the light of the world, broke through this darkened world, giving light to many, those accepting Yeshua the Messiah, the anointed one of God, therein are meant to reflect that light by also being a light in dark places.

But how can their light shine in dark places when their light only flickers?

How can truth emerge and branch forth when commingled with false teachings, as truth has nothing in common with lies?

Many believers of the faith are unaware that they are carrying baggage of false doctrine, and are being weighed down and enslaved by none other than their own hand, by having embraced certain teachings under the guise of being truth.

Consider the parable of the wheat and the tares. (*Matthew 13:24-30*)

---

11 The name Jesus is based on the Latin "Iesus," which is derived from the Greek "Ιησοῦς - Iesous," which is a derivative of the ancient Greek pagan name "Ζεύς - Zeus, a Greek mythological god." Which in Greek pagan mythology means "supreme god, protector and ruler of humankind." Why some languages insist on retranslating Biblical names to foreign pagan names, is deceptive at best. The Hebrew birth name for the Jewish Messiah is "ישׁוּע - Yeshua," it means "Gods Salvation."

At Matthew 1:21, Yeshua's name is used as a play on words, emphasizing the context of the story, something frequently found in the Hebrew language of the Bible. "You are to name him Yeshua (Gods Salvation) for he will Yoshia (Save) His people from their sins." Therefore, since the English name Jesus is derived from a pagan name, I will use his God given birth name Yeshua. However, in keeping the reading of this book from being intrusive, I will use the English translated names of the Bible for all other persons, while giving their Hebrew name once.

When these two plants are young they look similar in every detail, it is only upon closer examination and maturity that one is able to see the difference between the wheat, which has an edible light brown seed, whereas the tares have an inedible black seed, considered poisonous.
The tares having no value, it merely grows among the wheat absorbing its valuable nutrients and water, basically starving, injuring or killing off the good wheat.

The baggage of false teachings within the realm of believers is likened to that of the tares in a wheat field, choking and robbing vital nutrients for proper growth, damaging its integrity.

Approximately 3500 years ago, God lead the children of Israel "Out of Egypt (bondage)," before He judged that nation. Isn't it high time for the nations to come "Out of Babylon (confusion)" by letting go of baggage that serves only to enslave, before her judgment commences? For God surely will judge Mystery Babylon, the mother of whores and of the abominations of the earth.

This book, Out of Babylon Up to Jerusalem, is about coming out of man-made theologies that have and continue to this day to hold people in "bondage and confusion, the dark side if you will, masquerading as light." Although there are many man-made doctrines, this book only address' in-depth one of the many cultural tradition misconceptions, that being of the "so called" virgin birth theology. It would surprise, if not shock many Christians to discover that the Bible never teaches, promotes or justifies a virgin birth concept, in fact, the Bible teaches the very opposite.

Let me emphatically state that a virgin birth belief is "not a salvation document!" However, depending on one's belief, one will continue traveling down that said same road: the path of untruth or truth, or even that of a path commingled with both, which is still a perversion, as truth has nothing in common with lies.

The doctrine of a virgin birth is rooted in ancient Babylon, which is none other than Satan's realm, he being the father of all lies *(John 8:44)*. Its teachings are meant to distort and confuse the masses down through the ages, holding people in its tyrannical jaws with its upside down mindset.

Embracing and promoting a virgin birth doctrine is liken to that of a self-inflicted wound, as the Oldest Testament makes known the origin and personification of God's anointed one, the Messiah.
Whereas, the Newest Testament corroborates Yeshua's Messiahship, both Testaments must agree in every aspect!

We have on the one hand, Christians embracing a virgin birth, whereas, on the other hand for the Jewish people as a whole, it's a non-starter. And so, the great divide continues, one Bible, God's Word ripped in two, seemingly, never to be united, until now, this book "Out of Babylon Up to Jerusalem" will resolve for those willing to peer into its content "at least, the virgin birth issue," of a long overdue breach of the people of the one book.

Shouldn't Christians, of whom are also benefactors of God's kindness *(Romans 11)*, take the initiative in understanding why the religious Jew vehemently rejects a virgin birth concept, so as to actively participate in the Newest Testament directive; to bear witness of Yeshua as being the Jewish Messiah?

Wouldn't that be something to be a blessing to the Jewish people, just as they have been a blessing to the nations *(Genesis 12:2-3)*, namely, that of their faithfulness in their transmission of the Bible to all nations, that includes the Newest Testament, for they too, were all Jewish.

Wouldn't it be something to break down the middle wall of partition that has divided us for nearly two-thousand years, by removing the stumbling blocks, enabling the Jewish people to get past the first two chapters of the Newest Testament and onto the next round of qualifying factors in identification of their Jewish brethren, the Messiah?

With that said, let us now begin a verse by verse, in depth Scriptural analysis of text in question and its related subject, beginning our journey Out of Babylon, and into the promise land, Jerusalem.

Chapter Two

Yeshua's Genealogy / Messiah's Lineage

Matthew 1:1
> *This is the genealogy (origin) of Yeshua the Messiah (the anointed one of God), son of David, son of Abraham.*

The purpose of Matthew (Mattityahu) recounting the genealogy for Yeshua is so that believers that know the Scriptures (Oldest Testament) can be confident to place their trust in this person as being the anointed one of God, the Messiah.

For those seeking the Messiah, the genealogy given is but one of many signs to pay close attention to and evaluate its merit. As the Oldest Testament bears witness that the Messiah will be of the tribe of Judah (Y'hudah) *Genesis 49:10*, a son of David the king *2Samuel 7:12-16*, and a son of Abraham (Avraham) *Genesis 22:18*.

Yeshua's genealogy continues down to and through Joseph (Yosef), taking note that Yeshua's genealogy, as well as all genealogy throughout Scripture is consistently through the men, this is a fact that must not be ignored. In a later chapter, this subject will be discussed at length.

Rather than tediously review each and every one of Yeshua's ancestors of *Matthew 1:1-17*, this book will highlight only those ancestors that traditional Messianic and traditional Christianity deem as questionable.

From which, they then proceed to claim Luke's genealogy *(Luke 3:23-38)* as the needed link for Yeshua's Messiahship, only now, by conveniently forcing his mother Mary onto the pages of the text in order to place her lineage through the tribe of Judah and David the king, with the end goal being the removal of Joseph as Yeshua's biological father. Of course their claim is incongruous, a lot of manipulation has been done in order to arrive at this misguided and illogical conclusion. Their claim has serious problems and this too will be addressed at length in a later chapter.

Matthew 1:6

> *Jesse (Yishai) was the father of David the king. David was the father of Solomon (Shlomo) his mother was the wife of Uriah (Uriyah).*

Within traditional Messianic, it has been said that since Solomon (Shlomo) was cursed by God, that the lineage of the Messiah was removed from Solomon and given to David's other son Nathan (Natan) *(Luke 3:31)*. Thereby claiming Luke's genealogy *(Luke 3:23-38)* to now be the correct genealogy for the Messiah.

Curse of Solomon

1Kings 11:4-13

> *So it was that when Solomon grew old his wives turned his heart after the gods of others, so that he was not wholehearted with HASHEM his God as David his father had been. For Solomon followed Ashtoreth the goddess of the Phoenicians and Milcom the abomination of the Ammonites. Thus Solomon did what was evil in the sight of HASHEM, and did not fully follow HASHEM as David his father had done.*
>
> *Then Solomon built a high place for Chemosh the abomination of Moab on the hill (Mt. of Olives) in front of Jerusalem and one for Molech the abomination of the people of the Ammonites. He did likewise for all his foreign wives, who then offered and sacrificed to their gods.*
>
> *So HASHEM grew angry with Solomon because his heart had turned away from HASHEM the God of Israel, who had appeared to him twice and commanded him about this matter that he should not follow other gods. But he did not obey that which HASHEM had commanded him. So HASHEM said to Solomon, "since this has happened to you, and you have not kept My covenant and My decrees that I have commanded you, I will surely tear away the kingdom from you and give it to your servant. However, I won't do it in your lifetime, for the sake of your father David; I will tear it out of the hand of your son. Even then, I won't tear away the entire kingdom; I will give one tribe to your son for the sake of David My servant and for the sake of Jerusalem, which I have chosen."*
> *(See also 1 Kings 9:1-9)*

No doubt these verses written about Solomon later in his life were abhorrent. But the fact remains that there is not one verse in the entire Bible where God removes Solomon from the lineage of the future king, namely the Messiah.

One only needs to pay close attention to the words spoken in these verses to see just exactly what is being ripped away. Upon the death of Solomon, when his son Rehoboam (Rechav'am) takes reign, the kingdom of Israel and the kingdom of Judah will be divided. Rehoboam will only be king of Judah, not king of Israel: the northern tribes.

During David and Solomon's reign, both were kings collectively of Judah and Israel. It was a united monarchy in their day. But because of the sin of Solomon, the kingdom will now be divided in two when his son Rehoboam takes reign.

1Kings 11:31-32
> Then he (Ahijah/Achiyah) said to Jeroboam (Yarov'am), "Take ten pieces for yourself." For here is what HASHEM the God of Israel says: "I am going to tear the kingdom out of Solomon's hand, and I will give ten tribes to you."
> But he will keep one tribe[12] for the sake of My servant David and for the sake of Jerusalem, the city I have chosen from all the tribes of Israel.

1Kings 11:35-40
> However, I will take away the kingdom (of Israel) from the hand of his (Solomon's) son (Rehoboam) and give ten tribes of it to you (Jeroboam);. and to his (Solomon's) son (Rehoboam) I will give one tribe, so that there will always be a lamp for My servant David forever before Me in Jerusalem, the city where I have chosen to establish My name.
> I will take you Jeroboam, and you will rule over everything you desire; you will be king over Israel.
> Now if you will listen to all that I command you and live according to My ways, and do what is right in My view, to observe My decrees and My commandments as David My

---

12 The tribe of Benjamin was absorbed into the tribe of Judah. 2Chron. 11:12

servant did, then I will be with you and I will build a lasting dynasty for you, just as I built for David, and I will give Israel to you.
I will afflict the descendants of David for that sin, but not forever.
Solomon sought to kill Jeroboam, but Jeroboam roused himself, fled to Egypt, to Shishak king of Egypt, and he remained in Egypt until the death of Solomon.

Upon Solomon's death the united monarchy would become a divided kingdom, with Jeroboam ruling over the northern kingdom of Israel and Solomon's son Rehoboam ruling the kingdom of Judah to the south.
Although the united monarchy of Israel was divided after Solomon's death, this would prove to not be a permanent division. Jeroboam being wicked, had built the high places and initiated the kingdom of Israel (northern tribes) to go astray, therefore no lasting dynasty was set up for him.

As far as Solomon, "God will afflict the descendants of David for that sin, but not forever."
God's promise to David is an everlasting kingdom and this everlasting promise is based upon what God will do, not what David and sons do or don't do.

1Chronicles 17:10 ½-14
"Moreover, I tell you that HASHEM will build you (David) a house. When your days come to an end and you go to be with your forefathers, I will raise up after you one of your descendants, from among your sons, and I will establish his kingdom.
He will build a house (Temple) for Me, and I will establish his throne forever.
I will be a Father to him and he will be a son to Me, and I will not take My favor away from him, as I took it away from your predecessor (Saul / Sha'ul). I will establish him in My

house and in My kingdom forever, and his throne will be established forever."

The promise is made to David, reiterated through his son Solomon; the son who built the Temple (house) is the one the promised royal lineage will be through.
David's other son Nathan did not build the Temple, so it becomes apparent that Nathan is not the chosen son for the royal lineage. Nor is there any lengthy genealogy to speak of for Nathan, it is virtually silent other than him being one of David's many sons.
Most notable is that there is no mention anywhere in Scripture about a promise being made by God, to Nathan. Yet, David's lineage through his son Solomon, of which is through his son, etc., is amply documented.

Two-thirds of Yeshua's lineage in the book of Matthew can be traced directly from the Oldest Testament Scriptures, the remaining one-third genealogy happened after the Oldest Testament writings, and to the best of my knowledge it is untraceable. This is most likely due to the destruction of the Temple in 70 C.E.[13] (A.D.), where the scribes of the Temple would have kept those particular records, and where Matthew had possibly gained access prior to the Temple's destruction.
Of those two-third person's mentioned in Matthew's genealogy, there are several of those named in the Oldest Testament that the promise had been reiterated to them, by God.

To briefly name a few:

- Jehoshaphat (Y'hoshafat), David's third great grandson through Solomon: God established the Kingdom in Jehoshaphat hands. *2Chronicles 17:5*

---

13 C.E. Common Era.

- Jehoram (Y'horam), David's fourth great grandson through Solomon, even though Jehoram was evil: God was unwilling to destroy the house of David, because of the covenant He had made with David, and in accordance with His promise given to David and his descendants that a lamp would burn forever. *2Chronicles 21:7*

This is reiterated in the original words spoken about Solomon's son Rehoboam. *1Kings 11:35½-36*

- Hezekiah (Hizkiyahu), David's eighth great grandson through Solomon: God called Hezekiah, the ruler of My people. *2Kings 20:5*

From the following Scriptures, it is indisputable that Solomon had been the one chosen.

1Chronicles 22:9-10

> *But a son will be born to you (David), he will be a man of rest, and I will give him rest from all his enemies all around. His name will be Solomon, I will give peace and quiet to Israel in his days.*
> *He will build a house (Temple) for My name. He will be a son to Me and I will be a Father to him, and I will establish the throne of his kingdom over Israel forever.*

1Chronicles 28:4-9

> *HASHEM the God of Israel chose me (David) from all my father's family to be king over Israel forever. For He chose Judah to be the ruler, and in the house of Judah He chose my father's house, and among the sons of my father (Jesse) it was His pleasure to make me king over all Israel, and from all of my sons, for HASHEM has given me many sons, He has*

chosen my son Solomon to sit on the throne of the kingdom of HASHEM over Israel. He said to me, 'your son Solomon will build My house and My courtyard, for I have chosen him to be a son to Me, and I will be a Father to him. I will establish his kingdom forever, if he uses his strength to obey My commandments and abide by My rulings, as on this day.' So now, in the sight of all Israel, in the assembly of HASHEM, and in the hearing of our God, observe and seek out all the commandments of HASHEM your God, so that you may possess this good land and leave it as an inheritance to your descendants after you forever. As for you, Solomon my son, know the God of your father and serve him wholeheartedly with a willing soul, for HASHEM searches all hearts, and discerns all the inclinations of peoples thoughts.

If you seek Him, He will let Himself be found by you; but if you abandon Him, He will reject you forever.

If Solomon abandon's God, then God will reject Solomon, not the promised kingdom. The kingdom is an everlasting kingdom.

The "IF condition" here is whether they will possess, dwell in the land, "Possessing the land or living in Exile," if they observe God's word they will dwell in the land, if they disobey God's word they will be exiled, and even exile is only a temporary state, as the land of Israel was given to Abraham and his descendants forever by God. (*Genesis 13:14-16*)

Furthermore, one needs to read the above Scriptures along with its connecting Scriptures in order to understand the full content of what is actually being said.

2Samuel 7:11 ½-16

HASHEM declares to you (David) that He, HASHEM, will establish a house for you.

When your days come to an end and you sleep with your forefathers, I will raise up after you your offspring, one of

your own flesh and blood, and I will establish his kingdom.
He will build a house for My name, and I will establish his
royal throne forever.
I will be a father to him and he will be a son to Me, if he sins
I will punish him with the rod of men and with afflictions of
human being, but My grace will not leave him, as I removed
it from Saul, whom I removed from before you.
Your house and your kingdom will be made secure forever
before you; your throne will be established forever.

It was David's son Solomon that built the Temple, and it was through this same lineage that the royal throne was forever established. If Solomon sins, then God will punish him, the punishment of a king or the king's son who transgresses, will be a rebuke only "with the rod of men, and with the stripes of human beings," God's grace will never leave him, and the royal throne is established forever. The text only states that God will punish Solomon for his sin, not remove or reject the royal throne.

1Kings 11:35½-36

To his (Solomon's) son (Rehoboam) I will give one tribe, so
that there will always be a lamp for My servant David
forever before Me in Jerusalem, the city where I have chosen
to establish My name.

There will always be a lamp for God's servant David, it is established forever before God.
Throughout the collective verses, it is readily apparent that the royal lineage is through David's son Solomon, through his son Rehoboam, etc., in spite of their transgressions.

God left intact the tribe of Judah to Solomon's son Rehoboam. Just as God had spoken previously to Solomon, that upon his death, the kingdom would be a divided monarchy, with the kingdom of Israel (northern tribes) and the kingdom of Judah (the lamp), for He chose Judah to be the ruler. *1Chronicles 28:4*

Furthermore, we can see the "Remez and Sod" (hinting at, and the deeper contextual meaning) of these same Scriptural verses and see God's end goal, namely the Messiah, the anointed one of God, of whom it is written about, "Yeshua, the light of the world" God's lamp. *(John 8:12)*
It is God who is building the house, the Spiritual house, with Messiah as head of God's Kingdom, and God over all. *(1Corinthians 11:3, 15:23-28)*
The promise *(2Samuel 7:11-16)* that the Messiah will be one of David's descendants, through Solomon *(1Chronicles 22:9-10)*, that the future king, "King Messiah" will come. Not only will Messiah be King of Judah, but as well as King of Israel, a united monarchy, and King of all the nations, an everlasting kingdom. *(Isaiah 55:3-5)*

Additional Scripture
Reaffirming the promise to David through his son Solomon and sons.

God's word, God's promise to David is established forever in spite of some of David's descendant's sinful conduct, David's lineage moves forward as seen in the lineage of the book of Matthew *1:1-17.*

God's promise to David is reiterated through specific named descendants of David in the following verses.

1Kings 15:3-5

> *He (Abijam/Aviyam) committed all the sins his father (Rehoboam) had committed before him; he was not wholehearted with HASHEM his God, as his forefather David had been. Nevertheless, for David's sake HASHEM his God gave him a lamp in Jerusalem, by raising up his descendant after him and by preserving Jerusalem. For David had done what was right in the eyes of HASHEM, he had not turned away from anything He had commanded him to do all the days of his life, except in the matter of Uriah (Uriyah) the Hittite.*

1Chronicles 17:5

> *So HASHEM established the kingdom in his (Jehoshaphat) hands and all Judah gave tribute to Jehoshaphat, and he had wealth and honor in abundance.*

Here God established the kingdom into Jehoshaphat's hand. Jehoshaphat followed in the ways of his forefather David (third great grandson through Solomon). Not all of David's descendants were evil in the eyes of HASHEM. Nonetheless, just because some humans chose to do evil, in no way does their evil deeds abrogate God's promise. Humanity is dependant on HASHEM, God, the Creator and sustainer of life. To think otherwise, is like saying that God the Creator who created all things out of nothing, is now somehow dependant on the creation He created, this is an oxymoron.

2Kings 8:16½-19

> *Jehoram, son of Jehoshaphat king of Judah, became king. He was thirty-two years old when he began to rule, and he ruled eight years in Jerusalem. He followed in the ways of the kings of Israel, just as the house of Ahab (Ach'av) had done, for Ahab's daughter had become his wife; he did what was evil in the eyes of HASHEM. However, HASHEM was unwilling*

to destroy Judah, for the sake of his servant David, in accordance with His promise to give him and his descendants a lamp forever. (See also 2Chronicles 21:5-7)

Within these verses, it becomes apparent that in spite of the wickedness of Jehoram (Solomon's third great grandson), God is unwilling to destroy Judah for the sake of His servant David in keeping with His everlasting covenant to David. God never breaks His word He is trustworthy. God's lamp, the light of the world, has and will arise (Yeshua's first and second advent) according to God's word, in spite of some of David's descendant's evil conduct.

2Kings 19:34

(HASHEM speaking to Hezekiah king of Judah, through the prophet Isaiah (Yesha'yahu):
I will protect this city (Jerusalem), to save it, for My sake and for the sake of My servant David.

2Kings 20:4-6

Before Isaiah had left the city's middle courtyard, the word of HASHEM came to him: "Go back and tell Hezekiah, the ruler of My people 'Thus said HASHEM, the God of your forefather David; I have heard your prayer and seen your tears, and I will heal you. On the third day you are to go up to the house of HASHEM. I will add fifteen years to your life and I will rescue you and this city from the hand of the king of Assyria. I will protect this city for My sake and for the sake of My servant David.'"

God calls Hezekiah, the ruler (prince) of His people. In other words, God has chosen Hezekiah (a descendant of David, through Solomon). Also, God will rescue His chosen one and protect His city Jerusalem for His sake, as well as for

His servant David's sake, in whom the everlasting promise is made. The Davidic kingdom is secure forever and that end goal is Messiah Yeshua, God's anointed one, in whom the promised covenant is fulfilled, in keeping with the promise made to His servant David.

Jeremiah 23:5

> *Behold (interjection - to pay close attention to), days are coming says HASHEM, when I will raise up a righteous branch of David; he will reign as king and succeed, doing justice and righteousness in the land (earth).*

Luke 1:32-33

> *He will be great/mighty and called son of the Most High, and HASHEM, God, will give him (Yeshua) the throne of David his (fore-) father, (through" Joseph of the house of David" as identified in Luke 1:27) and he (Yeshua) will rule the house of Jacob forever/eternity, there will be no end to his kingdom.*

Yeshua is that righteous branch, as can be attested to from the pages of the Newest Testament. He is the one who has the key of David *(Revelation 3:7)*. He is the lion of the tribe of Judah, the root of David *(Revelation 5:5)*. He is the root and offspring of David, the bright morning star *(Revelation 22:16)*.

Yeshua's first advent was to atone for humanities sins[14], whereas his second advent will be to rule and reign as King, administering justice and righteousness in all the earth. There will be no end to his Kingdom. *(Luke 1:33)*

---

14 It is a hard concept for the Jewish people as a whole to accept that the Messiah would die in order to pay the price for humanities sins. Biblically speaking, the Israelites did in fact accept the sacrifice of lambs etc. as atonement for their sins. This particular subject will be addressed later in this book.

Chapter Three

Curse of Jeconiah/Coniah[15]

Within traditional Christianity, it has been said that since Coniah was cursed by God, that the lineage of the Messiah was removed from Coniah and given to David's other son Nathan *(Luke 3:31)*. Thereby claiming Luke's genealogy *(Luke 3:23-38)* to now be the correct genealogy for the Messiah.

Ironically, traditional Messianic removes Solomon, yet leaving Coniah intact. Whereas, traditional Christianity removes Coniah, yet leaving Solomon intact. Nonetheless,

---

15 In the Hebrew language of the Bible Y'khanyahu and Koniyahu collectively, has been translated into the English language Bibles a variety of ways: Jehoiachin, Jechoniah, Jechonias, Jeconiah and Coniah they are one in the same person. This book will use the English name Coniah in order to be less intrusive.

Scripture once again will prove that Matthew's lineage for the Jewish Messiah is the correct genealogy, of which is Yeshua's lineage.

Jeremiah 22:24-30

> *As I live, says HASHEM, even if you Coniah, son of Jehoiakim (Y'hoyakim/Eliakim) king of Judah were a signet ring on My right hand, I would pull you off. I will hand you over to those who seek your soul, into the hand of those you fear, into the hand of Nebuchadnezzar king of Babylon and into the hand of the Chaldeans. I will hurl you and the mother who gave birth to you into a different land where you were not born and there you will die. Therefore to the land, which their soul yearns to return, they will not return there. Is this man Coniah a despised shattered pot, an unwanted vessel? Why has he and his seed been displaced and hurled out into a land they do not know?*
> *O land, land, land! Hear the word of HASHEM!*
> *Thus said HASHEM: Inscribe this man as childless, a man not to succeed in his lifetime, that none from his seed will succeed as a man to sit on the throne of David and rule continuously in Judah.*

No doubt these verses written about Coniah were abhorrent. But the fact remains that there is not one verse in the entire Bible where God removes Coniah from the lineage of the future king, namely the Messiah. One only needs to pay close attention to the words spoken in these verses to see that God is exiling Coniah because of his increased distance from God's Torah.

The kings of Judah were to be shepherds, leaders teaching Gods ways, administering justice and righteousness in the land. The punishment for not shepherding the people was exile from the land, not elimination of the royal lineage.

From the following Scriptures we see exactly what happens to the children of Israel (king, priests and commoners alike) if they practice idolatry:

II Chronicles 7:19-22

> But if you turn away and abandon My decrees and My commandments that I set before you, and you go and worship the gods of others and prostrate yourselves to them, then I will uproot them from upon My land that I gave them, and this Temple that I have sanctified for My name I will cast out from My presence, and I will make it a parable and a proverbial saying among all the nations.
>
> And this Temple, which should be exalted, everyone passing by it will be shocked, and say, 'Why did HASHEM do this to this land and to this Temple?'
>
> And they will say, 'because they abandoned HASHEM the God of their (fore) fathers, who brought them out from the land of Egypt, and they coveted the gods of others, and they prostrated themselves and worshipped them; therefore He brought all this desolation upon them.'
>
> (See also Scripture I Kings 9:6-9)

So the punishment for idolatry was being uprooted from the land. Not, removal from the lineage of David, or Solomon whom God chose to sit on the throne and build His temple (1 Chronicles 28:5-7), or Jehoshaphat whom God established the kingdom in his hands (1 Chronicles 17:5), or Hezekiah whom God called the ruler of My people (II Kings 20:5), or Zerubbabel, (grandson of Coniah) whom God will make him like His signet ring and has chosen him (Haggai 2:23). God has reiterated His promise to all of these men mentioned above. Where Matthew has faithfully recorded Yeshua's genealogy for us, so that we could have yet another verifiable proof, that Yeshua is from the tribe of Judah, a descendant of David whom the promise was made.

A "Hebrew" key word in Jeremiah 22:30 is - "B' yama' v - בְּיָמָיו" Literally "in the life of him" in his life, better said would be "in his lifetime." So it becomes apparent that only Coniah is cursed and it is only during his lifetime.

Also in Jeremiah 22:30, where many English translators have chosen to translate the Hebrew word "od - עוֹד," as: again, anymore, yet, or no more, I felt as though none of the commonly used English words fully conveyed the true Hebraic meaning. In context of the story I felt that the English word "continuously" best reflected the underlining meaning of the Hebrew word "od - עוֹד." There are some Hebrew words that simply do not always transcend language, and therefore need further explanation, this being one such case.

> The Hebrew dictionary translates "od - עוֹד" as: repetition, duration, continuance, again, once more, continually, further, longer, still yet.

A general, but brief history needs to be conveyed first in order to get to the heart of the meaning of Jeremiah's prophecy. Just as there were previous eras formerly that had come and gone, so too in Jeremiah 22 a new era would emerge.

Previously, with the death of Joshua the Jewish nation would now enter into a new era. No longer was there a single national leader as Moses (Moshe) and Joshua (Y'hoshua) had been. After Joshua, the era of the Judges began. During this era, Israel sins by chasing after false gods, and therefore God punishes the people by subjecting them to foreign oppressors. Realizing their misdeeds, the people repent of their idolatry and pray to HASHEM for deliverance. HASHEM sends judges to rescue His people from the hands of the oppressors, and a tranquil period ensues. Some time after the death of the judges the people would lapse into idolatry and the cycle begins again. *(Judges 3:7-9, 12, 14-15; 4:1-3; 6:1,7)*[16]

So too would emerge a new era, the Jewish Monarchy (hereditary). There were righteous kings of Judah, but many were wicked, and there came a time when this era also needed to be dealt with in stopping them from their repeated vileness.

God having made an everlasting promise to David, the Davidic kingdom then would never cease.
Yet many of the kings of Judah were not administering justice and righteousness in the land, but rather were leading the people astray by polluting the land with such evils as idolatry. It then becomes obvious that these wicked kings would not continually sit on the throne of David ruling, repeating their vileness and leading the people astray. A new era would emerge, namely the kingdom would sit many days without a king.

Jeremiah 22:30 ½
that none from his (Coniah) seed will succeed as a man to sit on the throne of David and rule continuously in Judah.

Literally, none of Coniah's descendants has since sat on the throne of David as king continuously ruling in Judah. Since Coniah's captivity into Babylon, where he died, none of his descendants, to this day, has sat on the throne of David as king. The Scriptures only state: "continuously ruling," not his lineage ceases to exist, his lineage continues forward until arriving at the intended goal.

___

16 Encyclopedia Judaica

In other words, the throne of David would sit many days without a king, until the righteous king emerges, the Messiah, the anointed one of God, who we know is Yeshua, a descendant of David, through Solomon and sons, etc. It is this righteous branch, Yeshua the Messiah that will emerge at the end of this age, ushering in the everlasting kingdom.

In fact, many days, approximately 2600 years have passed since the children of Israel has had a king sitting on the throne of David, as prophesied:

Hosea 3:4-5

> For <u>many days the children of Israel will dwell without king</u>, *without prince, without sacrifice, without pillar, without ephod and teraphim. Afterwards, the children of Israel will repent and seek HASHEM their God, and David their king[17], they will come trembling to HASHEM and to His goodness in the <u>end days</u>.[18]*

The idea then behind Jeremiah 22:30; is that no longer would the kings of Judah sit on the throne of David continuously repeating wickedness and polluting the land with idolatry, king after king, after king, etc., no more than the former era of the Judges having ceased from the back and forth scenario of their day. Jeremiah 22:30; "od - עוֹד - continually" sitting on the throne of David does not mean that the lineage of the Messiah ceases through Coniah, but rather, the wickedness of these kings actions, will no longer be tolerated, they will cease from sitting in continuum on the throne of David, which is to be a seat of righteousness. There-

---

17 David their king, here refers to David's descendant, specifically the Messiah. See also Psalms 110:1

18 End days refers to the close of an age, when a new age is about to begin, here in context it's referring to the Messianic age.

fore the seat will be unoccupied; until the righteous heir to the throne emerges, namely the Messiah, the anointed one of God, as can be attested to in the adjoining chapter of Jeremiah 23:5, when God will raise up a righteous branch of David.

Jeremiah 23:1-8

> *Woe to the shepherds who lose and scatter the sheep of My pasture, says HASHEM. Therefore, thus (in consequence of) said HASHEM, God of Israel, concerning the shepherds who shepherd My people: you scattered My sheep, leading them astray, and not taken care of them. So I will take care of you according to your evil deeds – says HASHEM. And I will gather the remnant of My sheep from all the lands where I drove them, and there I will bring them back to their pasture and they will be fruitful and become numerous. I will establish shepherds for them who will shepherd them, and they will no longer be afraid, nor disgraced, nor afflicted, says HASHEM.*

> *Behold, days are coming says HASHEM, when I will raise up a righteous branch of David; he will reign as king and succeed, doing justice and righteousness in the land (earth).*

> *In his days Judah will be saved and Israel will dwell securely. This is the name by which he will be called: HASHEM is our righteousness.*[19]

> *Therefore, behold, days are coming, says HASHEM, when people will no longer say, 'As HASHEM lives, who brought the children of Israel up from the land of Egypt,' but rather,*

> *'As HASHEM lives, who brought up and brought back the offspring of the house of Israel from the land of the north and from all the lands where He drove them'; and they will dwell in their own land.*

---

[19] Psalms 118:26; Matthew 21:9; Mark 11:9-10; John 12:13

The day is coming when HASHEM, God, will raise up a righteous branch of David; he (the Messiah) will reign as King and succeed, doing justice and righteousness in the land. There will be a great ingathering when Messiah Yeshua returns and reigns as King, it will be a greater Exodus than that of the first Exodus out of Egypt (bondage), this second Exodus, per se, will be massive.

In the first Exodus there was a mixed multitude that came out of Egypt with the children of Israel *(Exodus 12:38)*, so too, will there be a mixed multitude at the second and greater Exodus (the ingathering/resurrection).

Yeshua the Messiah said this about the foreigner (mixed multitude) in reference to them joining the commonwealth of Israel:

John 10:16

> *Also I have other sheep which are not from this fold; I need to bring them, and they will hear my voice; and there will be one flock, one shepherd.*

HASHEM, God, said this about His righteous shepherd:

Ezekiel 34:23-24

> *I will establish over them a single shepherd and he will tend them - My servant David[20]; he will tend them and he will be a shepherd to them. I, HASHEM, will be their God; and My servant David (the Messiah) will be prince among them. I, HASHEM, have spoken.*

---

20 "My servant David" here refers to the Messiah, a descendant of David's. The Hebrew name David means, beloved of God.

HASHEM, God, through His prophet Isaiah, said this about the foreigners (mixed multitude) being attached to the house of Jacob:

Isaiah 14:1

> *For HASHEM will have compassion on Jacob - He will once again choose Israel and resettle them in their own land. The proselyte will join them and be attached to the house of Jacob.*

HASHEM, God, warning the foreigners (mixed multitude) to not separate from His chosen people:

Isaiah 56:3

> *Let not the foreigner, who has joined himself to HASHEM, speak, saying, "HASHEM will separate me from His people;" and let not the barren one say, "I am only a dried-up tree."*[21]

Childless / His Seed

Jeremiah 22:28-30

> *Is this man Coniah a despised shattered pot, an unwanted vessel? Why has he and his seed been displaced and hurled out into a land they do not know?*
> *O land, land, land! Hear the word of HASHEM!*
> *Thus said HASHEM: <u>Inscribe this man as childless</u>, a man not to succeed in his lifetime, that <u>none from his seed </u>will succeed as a man to sit on the throne of David and rule continuously in Judah.*

---

[21] See Romans 11:17-24, the parable of the olive branch and tree.

46

"Inscribe this man as childless"

I Chronicles 3:17
> *The sons of Coniah the captive: Shealtiel his son,*

We know from Scripture at Chronicles 3:17, that Coniah had at least one son, Shealtiel (Sh'altiel). Therefore *"inscribe this man as childless"* can then only refer to that of Coniah's son that would not sit on the throne of David in succession of Coniah.

Jeremiah 22:30
"None from his seed"

The Hebrew word "מִזַּרְעוֹ - me'zar'o" (from/of his seed), the identical word spelling found in Jeremiah 22:30 is found only four other times in the Oldest Testament at: Leviticus 20:2,3,4 and II Samuel 4:8, with each reference to: that man and his child or children, his offspring, his seed, and not that of his children's seed, meaning not his grandchildren. It refers specifically to "his seed" his children from his loins.

II Samuel 4:8 describes it best:
> *They brought the head of Ish-boshet to David in Hebron, and said to the king: "Here is the head of Ish-boshet, son of Saul your enemy, who sought your life. HASHEM has given my lord the king retribution this day from Saul and from his seed."*

Saul's son Ish-boshet having been the one killed, can then only be inferred as "his seed" to be none other than his child, and not that of any grandchildren.

Jeremiah 22:28 ½
> *Why has he and his seed been displaced and hurled out into a land they do not know?*

He (Coniah) and his seed (his children) having been displaced can only refer to Coniah and his children, because how do you *"hurl out"* future descendants not yet conceived or born?

Matthew 1:12 asserts an interesting word, where most translators have translated the Greek word "Μετὰ - meta" as "after."

> The Greek dictionary defines "meta" as:
> besides, afterwards, among, among them,
> with, together with.

The dictionary's overall definition "after / among" gives indication that Coniah's wife may very well have been pregnant upon their being hurled out of the land. Life begins at conception, thereby, Coniah's offspring *"he and his seed being hurled out."* Matthew having stated that Shealtiel was born, *"after the Babylonian exile,"* indicating that it was not long past the deportation.

Matthew 1:12
> *Now after the Babylonian deportation Coniah fathered Shealtiel*

Coniah being cursed only applied to Coniah, not the lineage nor future descendants lineage.

Zerubbabel, (grandson of Coniah) whom God will make him (Zerubbabel) like His signet ring and has chosen him *(Haggai 2:23)*, gives clear indication that the lineage moves forward, arriving at Yeshua the Messiah, of whom is the righteous heir to the throne of David.

The Holy Seed

Isaiah 6:11-13

> *I (Isaiah) then asked, "LORD (ADONAI), how long?" And He said, "Until cities become desolate, uninhabitable, houses without people, and the land becomes a desolate waste; for HASHEM will drive the people far away, and desolation will be great amid the land.*
> *There in it will continue ten (kings[22]), then lead away captive, then it (the land) will be consumed – But just as the vitality of the oak, after which when felled[23], the stump remains, so will the holy seed be the stock thereof."*

---

22 The word "Kings" is implied. The ten kings of Judah, starting with Uzziah (Isaiah 1:1) and ending with Jehoiachin/Jeconiah/Coniah (Jeremiah 22:30): 1- Uzziah 2- Jotham 3- Ahaz 4- Hezekiah 5- Manasseh 6- Amon 7- Josiah 8- Jehoahaz 9- Jehoiakim 10- Jehoiachin/Jeconiah/Coniah.

23 Felled - שׁלכת - Shallekhet, literally " cut down." Also, the name of one of the Temple gates in Jerusalem was called the "Shallekhet Gate" (I Chronicles 26:16), it was here that many oak trees grew and often in need of its branches or trunk being felled (shallekhet) as the oak tree having the ability to renew itself, therefore over-whelming the entry way. Here at Isaiah 6:13 the prophecy was a vivid picture describing the fate of the Jewish people, yet the stump having vitality, put forth the "holy seed," sprouting new shoots.

At the time of the prophecy of Isaiah, Judah would maintain its existence for about another 130 years before they would go into Babylon captivity. The prophecy here of Isaiah lines up perfect with Jeremiah 22, specifically verse 30. From the time of Uzziah (king of Judah) to Coniah (last king of Judah) there were exactly ten kings, then exile occurred and the land having become desolate of its people.

The imagery of the oak tree, is that the oak tree is long lived as well as hardy, the oak tree having the ability to renew itself, putting out new shoots from the stump or roots even though the tree has been cut down, yet no sooner was it felled, than the stump put forth seed, sprouting new shoots.

In short, Judah would be felled (exiled) yet this would not be permanent do to the holy seed in the stock (Messiah), which remains, renewing the vitality therein, as can be seen just a few chapters later in Isaiah 11:1.

Isaiah 11:1
> *A shoot (scion) will emerge from the stump of Jesse (Yishai[24])*
> *a branch will sprout from his roots.*

What's more, continuing through to Isaiah 11:2-5, these verses describe the righteous character traits of the Messiah, the King, the scion of David.

Whereas, the very opposite of these verses, had in reality reflected that of the majority of the previous kings of Judah in ancient days, of not having upheld justice. The majority of the kings of Judah were self-serving, which suppressed the people, not only of that of spiritual bondage, but as well as, eventually leading them into captivity in exile. While under the leadership of these kings of Judah who did evil from the

---

24 Jesse is king David's father, David is Yeshua's forefather, the promise is made to David and fulfilled in Yeshua.

perspective of HASHEM, God, the people were likened to a ship being tossed in a storm. There were a number of kings of Judah that were righteous and under their leadership the kingdom prospered spiritually as well as physically. However, upon their death, the kingdom would backslide, repeating an endless cycle.

Many events have and will occur prior to Messiah Yeshua's second and final advent, as can be attested to in the book of Revelation. The bottom line is that of the final restoration under one united and righteous monarchy; the righteous heir, the scion of David, King of kings and Lord of lords, Messiah Yeshua as head over the body, and HASHEM, God, over all, forevermore. (1Cor. 11:3)

Return from Captivity

After the Babylonia exile, as well as after Coniah's death, the children of Israel were told to return to Jerusalem to rebuild the Temple of God. Zerubbabel (Z'rubavel), grandson of Coniah, was in charge of the building of the second Temple, just as his forefather Solomon had been in the building of the first Temple, so too, will it be with their descendant; Yeshua the Messiah, the scion of David in the building of the third and final Temple of God. Of course, this third and final Temple of God being par excellence, entirely a Spiritual Temple, never to be uprooted, for Messiah Yeshua will be King, where HASHEM, God, will dwell in the midst of His people forever.

Zerubbabel became governor of Judah, but he was not sitting as king of Judah, just as had been prophesied that the kingdom would sit many days without king, until the righteous heir to the throne of David would come *(Hosea 3:4-5)*. Only then, when the righteous King comes at the end of this last age, at the ingathering of the saints for the greatest and final Exodus of all time, will then, the kingdom be reinstated as a united and everlasting monarchy.

Now one could reasonably argue, king or governor, isn't that basically the same thing considering its era?

Again, a new era has emerged. Flavius Josephus a first century historian states the following in Antiquities of the Jews, Book 11:111½ -112[25]

(These men, dwelling in Jerusalem) made use of a form of government that was aristocratical, but mixed with an oligarchy, for the high priests were at the head of their affairs, until the posterity of the Asamoneans (Hasmoneans) set up kingly government; for before their captivity, and the dissolution of their polity, they at first had kingly government from Saul and David for five hundred and thirty-two years, six months, and ten days: but before those kings, such rulers governed them as were called Judges and Monarchs (tribal chiefs). Under this form of government, they continued for more than five hundred years, after the death of Moses, and of Joshua their commander.

Zerubbabel led the people's return from Babylon exile, and was head over the rebuilding of the second Temple. But the government was no longer a monarchy, but rather, it was now a government made up of aristocratical and oligarchy members. In other words, it was known as the "Great Assembly" made up of one hundred and twenty wise and righteous members, it was the body that led the Jewish people during the early years of the Second Temple era.

---

25 The Works of Josephus, translated by William Whiston. Tenth printing - January 1995, Copyright 1987 by Hendrickson Publisher, Inc.

From the following verses, we see that Zerubbabel (son of Shealtiel and grandson of Coniah) was indeed chosen by God. Therefore it becomes quite obvious that although Coniah was cursed for his wickedness, his lineage was not cursed nor destroyed, because God had indeed chosen Zerubbabel, who was a grandson of the cursed Coniah.

Haggai 2:20-23

> *The word of HASHEM came a second time to Haggai (Hagai) on the twenty-fourth day of the month, saying, "Speak to Zerubbabel, governor of Judah, saying: I will shake the heavens and the earth. I will overturn the thrones of kingdoms and destroy the strength of the kingdoms of the nations, and overturn the chariots and its riders, horses and their riders will fall down, each by the sword of his brother. On that day, says HASHEM, Master of legions, I will take you Zerubbabel, son of Shealtiel, my servant, says HASHEM, and I will make you like a signet ring; for I have chosen you, says HASHEM, Master of legions."*

With regards to Haggai's prophecy, the Encyclopedia Judaica states that the prophecy against Coniah was now reversed.

> 'On that day (Kislev 24/December) the prophet (Haggai) told Zerubbabel that the LORD was about to shake heaven and earth, overturn kingdoms, and make him like a "signet ring" (*Haggai 2:18; 23*), thereby reversing the prophecy of Jeremiah against Jechoniah (Coniah).' (*Jeremiah 22:23*)

I certainly see their point, and find validity from that perspective. However, I also see it from a different view point, the words "reversing the prophecy" is troublesome, in light of the following Scriptures.

Numbers 23:19
> *God is not a man that He should be deceitful, nor a son of man that He should repent. Would He say and not do, or speak and not confirm?*

I Samuel 15:29
> *Moreover, the Eternal One of Israel does not lie and does not repent, for He is not a human that He should repent.*

Malachi 3:6
> *For I, HASHEM, have not changed; and you, sons of Jacob have not perished.*

Ps 89:35
> *I will not profane My covenant, and will not change what My lips have spoken.*

There is no need to "reverse the prophecy" about Coniah. The curse only "seemingly appears" to remove Coniah from the lineage of the future king (Messiah). As mentioned earlier in Jeremiah 22, the Hebrew word "od - עוֹד" means "continuously" ruling in Judah, not "ever again," therefore, there is nothing to reverse.

The point I'm getting at here is important, if as the Encyclopedia Judaica claims that God reversed the prophecy, or had changed His mind on this matter, then what's to say that God won't change His mind with any of the other promises He has made to us?
As the Scriptures state, God changes not, His word and His promises are set firm, God is completely trustworthy.

Therefore, the same is also true when God made a promise to David, reconfirmed it through Solomon, then Zerubbabel, ultimately leading to the Messiah, of whom, is of the said same lineage.

That what God said, He meant, in spite of what any of David's descendants do or don't do, it isn't what man will or will not do, but rather its what God said He would do!

Now what God did do was remove the kings of Judah from "continuously" sitting on the throne of David, and from polluting that throne any further, until the righteous heir to the throne of David comes.

Signet Ring: Reaffirmation of the Promise

A key word found in both prophesies of Jeremiah 22:24 and Haggai 2:23 is "Signet Ring."

Notice from Jeremiah 22:24 that God says that "if" Coniah were a signet ring of God's, God would pull him off. Whereas, in Haggai 2:23, God places Zerubbabel as a "Signet Ring," for God has chosen Zerubbabel.
Now in Biblical times, a signet ring never leaves the hand of its owner, it is his signature, his seal. Yet, the blessed Zerubbabel is the grandson of the cursed Coniah.

So obviously the curse is only:

1- During Coniah's "life-time."

2- His descendants would not sit "continuously" on the throne of David, violating the throne with their wickedness and injustices. Resulting directly to the throne sitting many days without king.

3- "Until the time would come, when God would raise

up a righteous branch of David," which is none other than Yeshua the Messiah, the anointed one of God.

Jeremiah chapter 22 must be read not only in context, but as well as, along side of Jeremiah chapter 23. Only then, when contrasting the two chapters are we able to see a vivid picture.

"A woe to the shepherds (kings) who lose and scatter the sheep of God's pasture."

In contrast to:

"When God will establish a righteous branch from David, a king who will administer justice and righteousness."

Continuing through the prophet Jeremiah, God confirms His word.

Jeremiah 33:15
In those days, at that time, I will cause a sprout of righteousness to sprout forth for David, and he will administer justice and righteousness in the land.

Additionally, through the prophet Ezekiel, God confirms His word.

Ezekiel 21:32
Desolate, desolate, desolate will I make it, such as there has never been, until he comes to whom justice belongs, I will established him.

The beginning of this verse is removing the wickedness from the kingship from ruling "continuously," where it will lie in ruin (without king).

Whereas the latter part of this same verse is that God will give the kingship of the throne of David to the righteous heir, the one who will do God's will, administering justice and righteousness.

So the Kingship has sat in ruin for approximately 2600 hundred years since Coniah, and it will continue to sit in ruin (without king[26]) until the righteous heir comes, the anointed one of God, Messiah Yeshua.

---

[26] Herod is an Idumean, hence he is not a descendant of Judah, David, Solomon et al., therefore he is not qualified to sit on the throne of David. Herod being a loyal subject of Rome, asked for the throne of Judea, the Roman senate, on the advise of Octavian and Anthony, proclaimed him king of Judea. Herod was a vassal of Rome.

Things aren't always as they appear

Zedekiah king of Judah was a vassal of Nebuchadnezzar king of Babylon *(2Chronicles 36:10)*.
Zedekiah was king of Judah after Coniah, but it was Nebuchadnezzar that had made Zedekiah king of Judah, not God. Also, Zedekiah was not Coniah's "descendant," but rather, he was his uncle, therefore Jeremiah 22:30 holds true; that "none of his (Coniah's) descendants will sit on the throne of David ruling continuously."

Even though Coniah was in captivity in Babylon, he was still called king of Judah until his death. Whereas Zedekiah (serving only 3 months) upon his captivity and exile, he was no longer called king of Judah.

Referring to the prophets Jeremiah and Ezekiel, it reminds me of an invaluable lesson learned while reading Scripture that detail is of vital importance.

In the Scriptures there appears to be a controversial prophecy about Zedekiah. Now the prophet Jeremiah had told Zedekiah that he would go into captivity in Babylon *(Jer. 39:4-7)*. Whereas Ezekiel had told Zedekiah that he would go into captivity, but that he would not see Babylon *(Ezekiel 12:1-14)*. Since both prophets of HASHEM, God, had said something "seemingly different" from Zedekiah's perspective, he thought that they were false prophets and therefore paid no attention to them, but rather he paid attention to the false prophets.

We know that both Jeremiah and Ezekiel were indeed true prophets of HASHEM, God. Therefore we must diligently consider each word spoken by these two prophets in order to resolve the "seemingly controversial" prophecy.

As the story of Zedekiah unfolds, we discover that Zedekiah was captured and taken to Riblah (northern border of Israel), there where Nebuchadnezzar was. At Riblah, Nebuchadnezzar, before Zedekiah eyes, had killed all his sons, and then plucked out Zedekiah's eyes, then placed in chains and taken into captivity in Babylon. Therefore, Zedekiah did indeed go into captivity in Babylon, but he did not "see" Babylon, just as both Jeremiah and Ezekiel had prophesied.

(See also II Kings 25:4-7)

Chapter Four

Luke's Genealogy

Having now reconciled Yeshua's genealogy in the previous chapters of this book, with that of Matthew's account to that of the Oldest Testament account; through David, Solomon, et al. to Zerubbabel, we must now turn to Luke's genealogy account. In this chapter we will begin utilizing some specific Greek words, as well as, compare two Greek text of the Newest Testament, along with the contrasting of English Bible versions, in order to better see what is actually being said in context.

In traditional Christian and Messianic[27] circles, many have claimed that; Luke's genealogy is that of Mary's

---

27 Christianity and Messianic are of the same school of thought, for ease of reading I will now only write the word Christianity when referring to both.

(Miryam's) forefathers, that Eli is Mary's biological father, and that Joseph (Yosef) therein mentioned is really the "son-in-law" of Eli (some English versions write Heli).

Let's take a closer look at two of the following Greek texts of Luke 3:23, with key words being highlighted in shadow, large bold italic font and underlined for easier viewing.

Byzantine/Majority Text[28]
και αυτος ην ο ιησους ωσει ετων τριακοντα αρχομενος ων ως ενομιζετο **_υιος_** ιωσηφ του ηλι

Novum Testamentum Graece[29]
Καὶ αὐτὸς ἦν Ἰησοῦς ἀρχόμενος ωσεὶ ἐτῶν τριάκοντα, ὢν **_υιός_**, ως ἐνομίζετο, Ἰωσὴφ τοῦ Ἡλὶ

With the exception of word order, these two Greek texts are identical in translation content, it does not affect the sense of the text in anyway.

The following two English Bible translations are of the preceding Greek text collectively.

NKJV[30] - Now Jesus Himself began _His ministry at_ about thirty years of age, being (as was supposed) _the_ son of Joseph, _the son_ of Heli,

---

28 Byzantine also called Majority Text, is the form found in the largest number of surviving manuscripts of the Newest Testament, though not the oldest, it also underlies the Textus Receptus Greek Text.
29 Novum Testamentum Graece normally refers to the Nestle-Aland editions (NA27 - 27th edition), named after those who led the critical editing work.
30 New King James Version copyright 1982 by Thomas Nelson, Inc.

NASB[31] - When He began His ministry, Jesus Himself was about thirty years of age, being, as was supposed, the son of Joseph, the son of Eli,

Now a literal English translation of the same Greek text:

Luke 3:23
> *Now Yeshua himself began to teach at about thirty years of age, it was supposed that he was a son (Greek - υἱός - "huios" – Hebrew - בֵּן -"ben") of Joseph, of Eli,*

First off the word "son-in-law" (Greek "Gambroi - γαμβροι" – Hebrew "Chatan - חתן") is not in the aforementioned Greek text, therefore it is not about a son-in-law.

Now the word that is used in the text is "son" (Greek "huios - υἱός" – Hebrew "ben - בֵּן") and it is applied to Yeshua as being a "supposed" son of Joseph, of Eli, etc.

One cannot superimpose "son-in-law" for the actual word used "son," no more than one could superimpose Mary's name for that of Joseph's name. By doing so, as traditional belief systems have done, only muddies the water.

Secondly, notice that the above English translations, or for that matter any English Bible translation, never once mentions Mary's name in the text of Luke's genealogy account.

Additionally, the fact that the word "son-in-law" is not in the text, further attest to that its not Mary's genealogy. Therefore it isn't about Mary, nor is it her genealogy as supposed by those within the traditional belief system.

---

31 New American Standard Bible copyright 1960, 1962, 1963, 1968, 1971, 1972, 1973, 1975, 1977, 1995 The Lockman Foundation.

Thirdly, traditional belief systems have mischaracter-ized the use of the word "supposed" in the text in order to claim that Yeshua had no earthly father. However, when rephrasing the text, as well as keeping it in context, it will simplify its intended meaning and purpose.

It was "assumed / supposed" (by some or many) that Yeshua was a son of (a certain) Joseph, (that was a son) of Eli.

Will the real Joseph please come forward.

Joseph, you know the one that is Mary's husband, that Joseph is a son of Jacob *(Matthew 1:16)*, not Eli *(Luke 3:23)*. So, it becomes apparent that Eli's son Joseph is an entirely different Joseph than that of the Joseph who is a son of Jacob.

Luke's genealogy account has absolutely nothing to do with Mary and Joseph, the parents *(Luke 2:27, 41,48)* of Yeshua, the one called Messiah *(Matthew 1:16)*. In fact, it has nothing to do with Yeshua either, other than stating plainly that "this is not Yeshua's genealogy," case in point "it was supposed/assumed," and that, is precisely the entire point that Luke is asserting to.

> It was "assumed," by others, that Yeshua the Messiah was a son of a "different" Joseph, who was a son of Eli, who was a son of Nathan, David's other son.

In other words, Luke is not arguing that Yeshua is a son of a Joseph, the argument lies with a Joseph who is a son of Eli, et al. Luke certainly knew the Oldest Testament Scriptures, and Luke would have known from those same Scriptures that the Messiah's lineage came through David, through Solomon, et al, through Zerubbabel. Anything short of that genealogy as can be attested to from the pages of the Oldest Testament, would promptly disqualify Yeshua as being the Messiah.

In Luke's day, just as in our modern day, or any given day in between, that unfortunately, rumors spread faster than a fire in a densely wooded forest.

Luke categorically, line by line, son to father, etc. places the "supposed" genealogy out there for all to see, to prove undeniably that there isn't any validity to this "supposed" genealogy.

In essence, Luke is throwing water on the fire before it gets out of control.

As a whole, every Jewish person, in every era, looks for the Jewish Messiah.

Any Jewish person considering Yeshua's eligibility as being the Messiah, only to discover "a rumor," of course not realizing that it is just a rumor, and if that rumor is believed, that Yeshua is:

1- A son of Joseph, of Eli, et al., Nathan.

2- Having no earthly father, as rumored by today's traditional Christian belief system.

Multitudes of Jews would have turned away from the real Messiah, based on a false rumor floating about, and by their doing so, would fall prey to, none other than a pseudo-Messiah. It sounds all so familiar doesn't it? Regrettably so!

So Luke needed to stop this false rumor in its tracks, before it could take hold, misleading the masses from obtaining their salvation, the very hope they sought. (Matthew 21:9; John 12:13; Psalms 118:25-26)

Nothing has really changed from Luke's day to our modern day, a rumor is still a rumor, and it has the capacity of burning out of control.

Have you noticed that Luke's genealogy account is in reverse order, youngest to oldest, son to father?

Nowhere in the entire Bible is a genealogy account done in a reverse order, except in Luke's genealogy account.

Just as Luke had intentionally written the word "supposed" in the text, he emphasized it by writing an "upside down" genealogy account, heightening his case in point.

So it becomes evident that Luke not only knew the lineage of Yeshua the Messiah, but he responded by acquiring Eli's lineage, no better way to counter a false rumor than to expose it openly for all to examine.

Any Jew, knowing Oldest Testament Scriptures with regard to the lineage of the Messiah, could promptly reveal from Luke's genealogy account, that it's a dead end street, and anyone accepting it as said, is barking up the wrong tree.

And that, is Luke's entire goal, stopping the ill-conceived rumor dead in its tracks, showing that something is awry, and he did it in four precise ways:

1- It was "supposed / assumed" - Not factual.

2- A reverse order genealogy account, son to father - Opposite of all Biblical accounts.

3- A different Joseph, that is a son of Eli, et al. to Nathan - No promise made, no kingdom established through Nathan, therefore ineligible lineage for the Messiah.

4- That Yeshua has a biological father named Joseph - just not of Eli, et al. Nathan.

Those doing gymnastics with the word "supposed" son of Joseph, while ignoring the "of Eli," in order to claim that Yeshua had no earthly father, have not considered the flaws within their own theory.

If, as supposed by traditional Christians that Luke's genealogy account is that of Mary's forefathers, then wouldn't this said same lineage also be of the same disqualifying factor for her, as it was for that of Joseph, of Eli, et al., Nathan?

The fact is, Nathan lineage, no matter whom it belongs, is an automatic disqualification as being the heir to the throne of David. Do you now see why Luke's genealogy account is not that of Mary and/or Joseph, the parents of Yeshua the Messiah, nor that of Yeshua himself?

Likewise, for anyone to claim Mary's lineage or Joseph as a son-in-law from Luke's text, is nothing other than taking deplorable liberties by; "adding words" to the original Greek text that otherwise does not exist, in order to make the text read according to their own imagination.

Taking such liberties is what is referred to as a "self inflicted wound," and one only needs to consider the following verses to grasp the point.

Deuteronomy 4:2
> *You are not to add to the word that I command you, nor are you to subtract from it, you are to observe the commandments of HASHEM, your God, that I command you.*

Deuteronomy 13:1
> *The entire word that I command you, you are to observe to do; you are not to add to it and you are not to subtract from it.*

Ecclesiastes 3:14
> *I know that whatever God does will endure forever; Nothing can be added to it and nothing can be subtracted from it, and God has done it so that we will fear Him.*

Revelation 22:18-19

> *For I testify to everyone hearing the words of the prophecy in this book, that if anyone adds to these things, God will add to him the plagues written in this book. And if anyone takes away (subtracts) from the words in the book of this prophecy, God will take away his share of the Tree of Life and the holy city, that are written in this book.*

The lineage of David, through his son Solomon, et al., through Zerubbabel, is the lineage that the Messiah will emerge from, as authenticated from the Oldest Testament.

Yeshua, himself states:

Revelation 22:16

> *I, Yeshua, have sent my messenger/angel to give you this testimony for the assembly (called out ones): "I am the root and offspring of David, the bright morning star."*

If, as supposed by traditional Christianity that Yeshua has no earthly birth father, then how is it possible for Yeshua to be a descendant of David? If, Yeshua has no earthly birth father, then how will Yeshua inherit the throne of his forefather David?

Birthright Inheritance

As far as Mary's genealogy, the only possible clue we have is somewhat vague, but nonetheless, it is an interesting remez (hinting at). Mary is a kinswoman (relative) of Elizabeth (Elisheva), who is a descendant of Aaron (Aharon) the high priest, of whom was born from the tribe of Levi. Zechariah (Z'kharyah), the husband of Elizabeth, is also of the priestly lineage of the tribe of Levi. Both, Zechariah and Elizabeth being from the tribe of Levi, and Mary being a relative of Elizabeth, (or even that of Zechariah), would make Mary most likely a descendant of that said same tribe of Levi. *(Luke 1:5, 36)*

A person's tribal affiliation is patrilineal. Thus, for example, a Jew with a father from the tribe of Judah and a mother from the tribe of Levi belonged to the tribe of Judah.

Numbers 1:2
> *Take a census of the entire assembly of the children of Israel, by their families of their fathers' household (ancestral tribe), by number of their names, every male according to their head count.*

Additionally, Scripture states:

Genesis 49:10½
> *The scepter will not depart from Judah, nor the ruler's staff from between his feet,*

Traditional Christianity, in spite of not having one shred of evidence, Biblical or otherwise; has claimed that Yeshua's birthright inheritance "the throne of David" is from his mother Mary, of which, they claim is from the tribe of Judah. Now, based on that said same school of thought, we would also have to take into account the other females listed in Yeshua's genealogy as having a birthright inheritance from his foremothers as well.

Matthew 1:1
> *"This is the genealogy of Yeshua the Messiah,"*

Two of the four women[32] listed in Yeshua's genealogy account, are:

  1- Tamar, a Canaanite
  2- Ruth, a Moabite

As a result of traditional Christian belief "female birthright inheritance," Yeshua would be that of Canaanite and Moabite descent, the same as that of his foremother's.

Now with regard to "female birthright inheritance," what will Yeshua inherit from his foremother's ancestral tribe? Certainly not the throne of David, as neither Tamar, nor Ruth is from the tribe of Judah.

Adhering to traditional Christian methodology; "The Scepter has departed from Judah, the rulers staff has departed from between his feet," turning Scripture upside down.

---

32 The other two women listed in Yeshua's genealogy are Rahab (Matthew 1:5) and Bathsheba (II Samuel 11:3; Matthew 1:6). There are no clear genealogies, or tribal affiliation for these two women. In fact, all four women listed have no genealogy to speak of, just snippets here and there, nothing substantial. Mary, although she is named in Matthews genealogy account, it is not her genealogy; it is her husband Joseph's lineage. Mary having no genealogy listed for her in any Biblical records, other than a hinting at the probability of her tribal affiliation to that of the tribe of Levite. Other than that, it's virtually silent.

Once again, *Genesis 49:10½*

> *The scepter will not depart* from Judah, *nor the ruler's staff from between his feet,*

Notice that Scripture reads "his feet" not "<u>HER</u> feet."

The very thing that traditional Christianity claims, that Yeshua's genealogy birthright inheritance is through his mother; is in fact the very thing that would remove Yeshua from inheriting the throne of David, as descent for purposes of inheriting kingship cannot be counted through the mother.

We know that David is from the tribe of Judah, yet David's foremother's are, Tamar a Canaanite and Ruth a Moabite, yet no one doubt's David's genealogy birthright authenticity of being of the tribe of Judah.
So how is it possible that David is of the tribe of Judah when his foremother's are of foreign descent?

In every Biblical genealogy account, birthright inheritance is passed on from father to son; this is how the birthright of each of the twelve tribes of Israel attributes to their own collective tribes. It works the same way for David the king, his father before him is of the tribe of Judah, etc., and his son after him is of the tribe of Judah, etc., irrespective of what tribal affiliation his mother or foremother's are from.

Matthew being true to form in his genealogy account, father to son, he does not suddenly change direction or veer off course when he accounts for Yeshua's birth and birthright inheritance. Matthew is on a mission to prove unequivocally that Yeshua is a qualified descendant of David and that Yeshua is in fact, the Messiah, the anointed one of God.

Joseph's Lineage

The angel of HASHEM declared Joseph's lineage:

Matthew 1:20
> *Joseph, son of David.*

Luke 1:32-33,
> *He (Yeshua) will be great/mighty and called son of the Most High, and HASHEM, God, will give him (Yeshua) the throne of **his forefather David** (through "Joseph of the house of David" as identified in verse 27;) and he (Yeshua) will rule the house of Jacob forever, there will be no end to his kingdom.*

God Himself sends His angel to declare a message, and while doing so, he points out a pertinent fact, that Joseph is a qualified descendant of David's, of which, qualifies Yeshua as a legitimate heir to the throne of David, so, who are we to argue God's message or correct God's grammar? (*Romans 11:34*)

If, as supposed by traditional Christianity that Yeshua has no human birth father, then why does Scripture bother with emphasizing Joseph's status as being of the house and lineage of David?

If Joseph's lineage is irrelevant to Yeshua's origin of birth and that of his birthright inheritance, then why does Scripture so frequently point out Joseph's connection to that of David?

If, as supposed by traditional Christianity that Yeshua has no human birth father, then Yeshua has no claim to David's throne. One can't have it both ways.

Matthew also points out that Joseph went up to Bethlehem for a census because Joseph is a descendant of David.

Luke 2:4
Joseph of the house and lineage of David

Note what all of the aforementioned Scriptures do not say:

It does not say:

> 1- Mary, daughter of David
> 2- Mary, of the house of David
> 3- Give him (Yeshua) the throne of his
>   mother/foremother
> 4- Mary of the house and lineage of David

Nowhere in Scripture does it ever mention Mary being of the tribe of Judah, or a descendant of David.

Emphasis has been placed on Joseph as factually being a direct descendant of David the king, through Solomon, etc. It is through this physical lineage of David, that HASHEM, God, will give the throne of David to one of David's physical descendants, namely Yeshua.

In both books of Matthew and Luke both writers take the time to single out and validate that Joseph is a descendant of David the king, it is as if they had taken out an ad, placed it on a huge billboard in huge bold letters for the world to see when passing by:

"Joseph, son of David"

"Joseph, of the house and lineage of David"!

Additionally,

John 1:45

> *Yeshua son of Joseph from Nazareth (Natzeret)!*

John 6:42

> *Isn't this Yeshua the son of Joseph, whose father and mother we know?*

Luke 2:41

> *His (Yeshua's) parents*

Luke 2:48

> *Your (Yeshua's) father and I have been grieved with worry looking for you.*

Now, there are some within traditional Christianity that has also claimed that Joseph adopted Yeshua. Hogwash! There isn't one shred of evidence to support this imaginary theory. If Scripture wanted to say that, it could have easily added the word "adopted" to the text by simply saying, Yeshua the adopted son of Joseph, but it didn't say that, because it's not factual!

Scripture certainly is not silent as to who Yeshua's human birth father is, there is ample evidence that supports Joseph as Yeshua's birth father.

If, as supposed by traditional Christianity that Yeshua has no human father, then how can Yeshua be a descendant of the very human David? It is through human ancestry that Yeshua, himself human, can be a descendant of David, human father to human son, etc.

Can a bear give birth to a lion, or a pigeon give birth to an eagle?

1 Timothy 2:5

> *For God is one, and there is but one mediator between God and humanity, Messiah Yeshua, himself human,*

1 John 4:2-3

> *This is how you recognize the Spirit of God: every spirit who acknowledges that Messiah Yeshua came as a human being, is of God, and every spirit that does not acknowledge that of Yeshua, is not of God, this is of the anti-messiah, which you have heard was coming, well, even now, is already in the world.*

2 John 7

> *For many deceivers have gone out into the world who do not acknowledge Messiah Yeshua as coming as a human being. This is a deceiver and an anti-messiah.*

No doubt, with these verses, traditional Christianity, already prepared with their answer to explain their belief, all having agreed that Yeshua is 100% human, but they don't stop there, they go on to claim that Yeshua is also 100% God. Of course, there isn't any supporting evidence from the Bible to support their theory. It is only by manipulation of the text, by adding and subtracting words, their forcing of the text to say what they want it to say.

The above verses state only, that Yeshua is a human being, nowhere in these verses does the text state in addition to Yeshua being human, that he is also God.

In fact, 1 John specifically states how to recognize the Spirit of God, and that is that Yeshua is a human being, and anyone who claims more than what the text states, something other than, something different than Yeshua as a human being is; of the anti-messiah.

In short, anyone professing that Yeshua is 100% God, is a deceiver, and is of the anti-messiah.

If, as supposed by traditional Christianity that Yeshua is God, then why would God, as a mediator stand between Himself and humanity? How many God's are there?

1 Timothy 2:5 states; "God is ONE, and there is but one mediator between God and humanity, Messiah Yeshua himself human," clearly a distinction between the two.[33]

Now, traditional Christianity will profess, they believe that God is One. But again, they don't stop there, they go on to also claim that in this one is three, God the Father, God the Son, and God the Holy Spirit, in short its called a trinity, more moderns are now calling it a tri-unity, just a play with words, its the exact same thing with the exact same meaning.

In traditional Christian thought, their world of math,
$$1+1+1 = 1$$

Again, there isn't any supporting evidence from the Bible to support their theory, or their math wizardry.

---

[33] I Sam.15:29, Eph. 5:23, Col. 1:18, 2:19, 1Cor. 15:24-28. Paying particular attention to 1Cor. 15:27-28; that God has subjected everything under the Messiah's feet, but when it says "everything" has been subjected, obviously it does not include God, who is Himself the one subjecting everything to the Messiah. Hence, Yeshua is not God; Yeshua is subject to God, verse 28.

The Hebrew word for one is, "אֶחָד - Echad," it literally means; one, a single one.

It is the exact same word used by Israeli's for the number one.

Echad + Echad + Echad = Sh'loosh (three)

Hebrew is read from right to left

שְׁמַע יִשְׂרָאֵל יְהוָה אֱלֹהֵינוּ יְהוָה ׀ אֶחָד   *Deut. 6:4*

Deut. 6:4
Hear Israel, HASHEM is our God, HASHEM is Une.

HASHEM alone is God! The human race is to acknowledge and be a witness to this very fact! It is factually the most important commandment of all!

Yeshua acknowledged that HASHEM alone is God.

Mark 12:28
One of the Torah-teachers came up, having heard them in conversation. Seeing that Yeshua had answered them well, he asked him, "Which is the most important commandment of all?"

Mark 12:29
Yeshua answered, "The most important is:
Hear Israel, HASHEM is our God, HASHEM is One."

Mark 12:32
The Torah-teacher said to him, "Well said, Rabbi; you speak the truth that HE is One, and there is no other, only HIM."

Mark 12:34
Yeshua saw that he answered wisely, he said to him, "You

are not far from the Kingdom of God." After that, no one dared to question him anymore.

If, as supposed by traditional Christianity that Yeshua is God, then Yeshua missed a golden opportunity in the above verses to claim deity. Yeshua could have easily said, "Hear Israel, HASHEM is our God, HASHEM is One" and by the way folks, that's me, I'm God in the flesh, I'm one of the three but we're really just one! But no, Yeshua didn't say that, because there was no missed opportunity, because what traditional Christianity claims simply isn't factual!

When Yeshua was asked, "Which is the most important commandment of all," Yeshua himself proclaimed that there is no greater commandment than:

"HASHEM is <u>our</u> God, HASHEM is One!"

In so doing, Yeshua himself, leaving no shadow of a doubt to his own conviction of faith, that HASHEM is <u>OUR</u> God, i.e. - <u>his</u> God. Yeshua didn't say: HASHEM is <u>YOUR</u> GOD!

Even the Torah-teacher had made known that Yeshua spoke the truth that God is One and there is no other, HASHEM alone is God! And what was Yeshua's response to the Torah-teacher, affirmation that he got it right, that he is heading in the right direction, by telling him that he is not far from the Kingdom of God!

Yeshua declared that God, is <u>his</u> God:

John 20:17

Yeshua said to her, "Stop holding onto me, because I have not yet ascended to the Father, but go to my brothers, and tell them that I am ascending to my Father and your Father, to <u>my</u> God and <u>your</u> God."

From the following Scriptures notice what is said, as well as what is not said, it is very telling.

Revelation 17:14 ½
> *They will wage war with the Lamb, but the Lamb will defeat them, because he is Lord of lords and King of kings.*

Deuteronomy 10:17 ½
> *For HASHEM your God, HE is God of gods, and LORD of lords, the great, mighty, and awesome God.*

It is paramount to note that Revelation 17:14 does not say that Yeshua (ישוע) is God of gods! The text of Revelation states only that Yeshua is: "Lord of lords and King of kings," indicating his title of Messiahship, the anointed one OF God.
On the other hand, Deut 10:17 unequivocally states that "HASHEM (יהוה) alone is GOD, HASHEM is GOD of gods and LORD of lords." LORD of lords indicates HIS title of Supreme Sovereignty.
HASHEM alone is God; there is no other God besides HASHEM.
(Deuteronomy 4:16; 5:7)

There is a huge difference with the English words "**LORD**, Lord and lord;" although difficult to discern the difference in the English language Bibles, most Bible readers never tune into those particular nuances.
Most English translators, when translating the Hebrew Name יהוה of God, are not literally translating HIS NAME, but rather they are substituting HIS NAME as LORD. In so doing, they capitalize each English letter as: LORD.
When referring to Yeshua ישוע they capitalize only the first letter as in: Lord. When referring to all others, no capitalization is done as in: lord.

Just as there is a difference in the English translations, which is derived from the Hebrew language, and most importantly there is a huge difference in the Hebrew language of the words: ADON<u>AI</u> - <u>LORD</u>, Adon<u>ee</u> - <u>L</u>ord, or adon<u>eem</u> - lords (adon<u>eem</u> is merely the plural of adon<u>ee</u>).

In the Hebrew language the difference is Not the subtle Capitalization of letters, but rather it is the word itself and its proper pronunciation of the Hebrew words that make the difference.

The Hebrew root word for "ADONAI, Adonee/m" is "Adon - אדון," <u>it is a "Title."</u>

The Hebrew dictionary translates "Adon - אדון" as: Lord, master, ruler, commander, Mr., sir, owner, possessor, proprietor, head of household.

In context of our subject Scriptures;

Revelation 17:14;
    Yeshua is <u>L</u>ord (Adon<u>ee</u>) of lord<u>s</u> (adon<u>eem</u>).

Where as, *Deuteronomy 10:17;*
    HASHEM, God, is <u>LORD</u> (ADON<u>AI</u>) of lord/s (adon<u>ee</u>/<u>m</u>).

The proof is in the text:
Revelation 17:14 Yeshua (ישוע) is: "Lord (Adon<u>ee</u>) of lords (adon<u>eem</u>) and King of kings" in contrast to that of:

Deuteronomy 10:17 "HASHEM (יהוה) your God, HE is God of gods, and LORD (ADON<u>AI</u>) of lords (Adon<u>ee</u>/adon<u>eem</u>)."

Notice that Revelation does not say "God of gods," i.e. Yeshua (ישוע) is not God! Only HASHEM (יהוה) is God!

Abraham, Moses, David, Elijah and many more, were called "lord - adonee," no one would misconstrue them of being God when they were called lord.
(*Genesis 18:12, Genesis 23:6, Numbers 11:28, 2Samuel 4:8, 1Kings 18:7*)

HASHEM, God, has made Yeshua "Lord/Adonee and Messiah:"

Acts 2:36
> *Therefore, let the whole house of Israel know assuredly that God has made him Lord and Messiah, Yeshua, this one whom you crucified.*

If, as supposed by traditional Christianity that Yeshua is God, then why is there an obvious distinction between God, the One who bestows, and Yeshua, the one who is the recipient?

Yeshua comes in the Name of the LORD, not Yeshua is the LORD! Yeshua is a representative of HASHEM GOD (*Mark 11:7-10*). Yeshua is the mediator, the one standing in the gap that paid the price for humanities sins, in order to reconcile humankind to HASHEM God.

Yeshua never claimed that he is God, or God of gods[34]!

Yeshua himself did claim Davidic lineage:

Revelation 22:16
> *I, Yeshua, have sent my messenger/angel to give you this testimony for the assembly (called out ones): "I am the root and offspring of David, the bright morning star."*

---

[34] For an excellent and in-depth study of the Non-trinity, see: www.torahofmessiah.org

Others acknowledged Yeshua as a son of David:

Mark 10:47
> *When he heard that it was Yeshua of Nazareth, he called out,*
> *" Yeshua, son of David, have mercy on me."*
> *(also see: Mt. 9:27, Luke 18:38, Romans 1:3-4, 2Timothy 2:8)*

Zechariah proclaimed:

Luke 1:68-69
> *Praise be HASHEM, the God of Israel, because He has*
> *visited and made a ransom for His people, by raising up a*
> *mighty deliverer for us from the house of His servant David.*

A scene within the Heavenly throne room:

Revelation 5:5
> *One of the elders said to me, don't lament. Look, the Lion of*
> *the tribe of Judah, the root of David, has won the right to*
> *open the scroll and its seven seals.*

Yeshua referred to himself numerous times as a "Son of Man." Son of Man - Hebrew בֶּן־אָדָם - ben a'dam, literally "son of Adam" simply said, "a descendant of the human race, mankind."

John 5:27
> *… and has given him authority to execute judgment, because*
> *he is the son of man.*

John 6:27
> *Don't work for the food that perishes, but for the food that*
> *continues on into eternal life, which the Son of Man will give*
> *you, because on him, God the Father has placed His seal.*

HASHEM calls Ezekiel numerous times, a Son of Man:

Ezekiel 3:17
> *Son of Man, I have appointed you to be a watchman for the house of Israel, when you hear a word from My mouth, you are to warn them on My behalf.*

No one would ever consider Ezekiel when being called a "Son of Man" as to not being human, or as one not having an earthly birth father, so why would anyone dismiss Joseph as Yeshua's natural birth father, when Yeshua himself attest that he is a "Son of Man" a human being?

If, as supposed by traditional Christianity that Yeshua has no earthly flesh and blood human birth father, then what is the point of Scripture stressing the fact that Yeshua is a descendant of David's, a descendant that would inherit the throne of his forefather David?

Or, if as supposed by traditional Christianity that Mary is somehow from the tribe of Judah and that's how Yeshua inherits the kingdom, then what is the point of Scripture stressing Joseph's lineage as a son of David, and being silent about Mary's lineage?

Or, what would be the point of Matthew tediously listing each physical descendant of Yeshua's forefathers, from Abraham to Joseph, just to disqualify Joseph and the whole lot of them in the end? Has Matthew nothing better to do with his time, than to confuse and play head games with the masses?
Why then would Matthew bother with the long arduous genealogy? The entire point of Matthew meticulously writing this line by line genealogy, is so that the reader can trust that Joseph, from the physical lineage of king David, through Solomon, et al., of the tribe of Judah; qualifies his physical descendant Yeshua as a legitimate valid heir to being the long

awaited Messiah, the anointed one of God. Yes, it really is that simple.

From the beginning of Matthew's discourse, he plainly states that:

Matthew 1:1
> *This is the genealogy of Yeshua the Messiah, son of David, son of Abraham:*

Followed by a long list of Yeshua's ancestry, from father to son etc., all the way to, and through his biological birth father Joseph. It would behoove us to take Matthew at his word, that this is Yeshua's genealogy, because it is this genealogy that qualifies Yeshua as the legitimate heir to the throne of David, Matthew's very point.

At Matthew 1:16, somehow by this verse traditional belief systems have come away thinking that Joseph was merely Mary's husband after the fact, that Joseph had nothing to do with her pregnancy. We will be dealing with this issue in far greater depth, but first let's finish up with Yeshua's genealogy through Joseph.

Matthew 1:16 has two pivotal Greek words, they are highlighted in shadow, large bold italic font and underlined for easier viewing.

Byzantine/Majority Text
ιακωβ δε εγεννησεν τον ιωσηφ τον ανδρα μαριας *εξ ης* εγεννηθη ιησους ο λεγομενος χριστος

Novum Testamentum Graece
Ἰακὼβ δὲ ἐγέννησεν τὸν Ἰωσὴφ τὸν ἄνδρα Μαρίας, *ἐξ ἧς* ἐγεννήθη Ἰησοῦς ὁ λεγόμενος χριστός.

Now two English translations of the previous Greek text:

NKJV - And Jacob begot Joseph the husband of Mary, <u>of whom</u> was born Jesus who is called Christ.

NASB - Jacob was the father of Joseph the husband of Mary, <u>by whom</u> Jesus was born, who is called the Messiah.

The two pivotal Greek words:

("ἐξ - ex or ek ") This Greek word is defined as:
the point where motion or an action proceeds, out of, from among, from, immediately after; on the part of, because of, in consequence of.

("ἧς - hes") This Greek word is defined as:
to express result or purpose, who, which, that, this, he, she, it.

With those two pivotal Greek words in mind, lets now translate Matthew 1:16

Matthew 1:16
    Jacob was the father of Joseph, the husband of Mary, <u>out of it</u> (this union) was born Yeshua, called the Messiah.

Said another way: Joseph, the husband of Mary, out of whom (both father and mother) was born Yeshua, called the Messiah. In other words, these two pivotal Greek words are dependent upon each other in relationship, together collectively, something that preceded the birth of Yeshua but is also the result of that birth. This being Joseph and Mary's union, from this union is born Yeshua.

From the Greek Septuagint[35], Genesis 3:19 uses the exact same Greek pivotal words:

---

35 The Septuagint (LXX) is an Ancient Greek translation of the Hebrew Bible (Oldest Testament). The translation process was undertaken in stages, beginning 3rd century B.C.E. and completed by 132 B.C.E. Before Common Era.

ἐν ἱδρῶτι τοῦ προσώπου σου φάγῃ τὸν ἄρτον σου ἕως τοῦ ἀποστρέψαι σε εἰς τὴν γῆν **ἐξ ἧς** ἐλήμφθης ὅτι γῆ εἶ καὶ εἰς γῆν ἀπελεύσῃ

Where most English translators have chosen to translate Genesis 3:19 "ἐξ ἧς[36]" as: "out of it."
Yet, from Matthew 1:16, most English translators translate "ἐξ ἧς" as: "of whom."

By selection the use of the words "of whom" makes Scripture less clear, a subtle way of making it appear as though Joseph had nothing to do with Mary's pregnancy, by making it appear to apply to Mary alone. Whereas, "out of it" clarifies Scripture of its intended meaning, that Joseph and Mary "out of it" both persons, their union, was born Yeshua, called the Messiah.

Additionally, there is another specific Greek word used in Matthew 1:16, the word "husband" ("ἄνδρα °- andra.") Joseph is Mary's husband, not her betrothed, and it is this union of Joseph and Mary that conception began, they being married, living as a married couple.
Had Joseph and Mary not consummated their marriage, then they would have still been in the betrothal stage.

---

36 The Greek words "ἐξ ἧς" can also be found in the Greek Septuagint of the Oldest Testament at: Gen 3:23, Amos 5:3 twice, Jer 2:11, Macc 1:19, Wis 15:8, and in The Works of Josephus: Antiquities of the Jews 1:238; 2:107, 3:143, 5:214, 6:67, 6:251, 7:168, 7:383, 8:201, 12:160, 13:69, 14:121, 14:300, 17:19, 17:320, 18:307, 20:23, 20:149, and Wars of the Jews 1:241, 1:337, 1:503, 4:504, 4:559, 7:173. Whereby translators have translated these two Greek words in a variety of ways: out of, out of it, out of which, out of whom, out of that, from it, from whom, from which, by whom, by that, of whom, of them, of this, to which, that which, forth from, etc.

If the Greek text wanted us to believe that they had no sexual union, they could have simply used the word betrothed, "ἐμνηστευμένην᷉ - emnesteumenen," and said "Joseph the betrothed of Mary," but the text doesn't say that. But rather the text is being specific to say "Husband of Mary," followed by the Greek words "ἐξ ἧς - ek or ex – hes," denoting where the motion or actions proceeds, and the result of that union, was born Yeshua, a physical descendant of Abraham, Isaac, Jacob, Judah, David, Solomon, Zerubbabel and Joseph.

Disqualifying Joseph also disqualifies his entire forefather's; in so doing, the end result is that Yeshua would not be a qualified candidate to being the Messiah.

What would the point be of Matthew meticulously giving Yeshua's lineage through Joseph, if only in the end to disqualify all 42 generations?

The genealogy in Matthew is the genealogy of Yeshua, from the tribe of Judah, from the lineage of David the king, through Joseph.

It is this lineage of David, that HASHEM, God, ordained to be an everlasting kingdom. This is why Matthew tediously listed each of Yeshua's physical forefathers, as one of many signs, so that the reader could have confidence that Yeshua is the one prophesied about, and is indeed the long awaited Messiah.

Chapter Five

<u>Joseph's Character - Matthew 1:18-21</u>

Taking a look now at two popular Bible translations of the book of Matthew, chapter one verses 18 through 21.

NKJV Matthew 1:18 - 21

18- Now the birth of Jesus Christ was as follows: After His mother Mary was betrothed to Joseph, before they came together, she was found with child of the Holy Spirit.

19- Then Joseph her husband, being a just *man*, and not wanting to make her a public example, was minded to put her away secretly.

20- But while he thought about these things, behold, an angel of the Lord appeared to him in a dream, saying, "Joseph, son of David, do not be afraid to take to you Mary your wife, for that which is conceived in her is of the Holy Spirit.

21- And she will bring forth a Son, and you shall call His name JESUS, for He will save His people from their sins."

NASB Matthew 1:18-21

18- Now the birth of Jesus Christ was as follows: when His mother Mary had been betrothed to Joseph, before they came together she was found to be with child by the Holy Spirit.

19- And Joseph her husband, being a righteous man and not wanting to disgrace her, planned to send her away secretly.

20- But when he had considered this, behold, an angel of the Lord appeared to him in a dream, saying, "Joseph, son of David, do not be afraid to take Mary as your wife; for the Child who has been conceived in her is of the Holy Spirit.

21- She will bear a Son; and you shall call His name Jesus, for He will save His people from their sins."

After reading these or any English Bible translation, it isn't surprising as to why traditional Christians believe what they do; that being that "Mary was with child of/by the Holy Spirit before she and Joseph came together."

However, English translations of the above verses are at odds with their own translation, and do not make sense in context when read in its entirety.

On the one hand, English translations of Matthew 1:18 has Mary pregnant, yet on the other hand in the very next verse of Matthew 1:19, it has Joseph not willing to disgrace and make Mary a public spectacle, all the while in secret.
If, as supposed by traditional Christianity that Mary was actually pregnant at this juncture, then wouldn't Joseph in fact

be doing what Scripture explicitly states that he doesn't want to do; disgrace and make Mary a public spectacle by releasing her from the marriage contract when she is pregnant?

In a few short months her pregnancy and her unmarried status will be headline news, how much more disgraced could a woman in her culture be than to be pregnant and unmarried?

Scripture states that Joseph is righteous, yet we are to believe that this righteous man is going to secretly put or send a pregnant woman away without the end result of her being humiliated and publicly disgraced?

No doubt, some within traditional Christianity will say that Joseph's thoughts were only temporary, after the angel had visited him, he ended up not doing what he was contemplating, so all's well that ends well.

Well not so fast, in Biblical Hebraic thought, a woman that was betrothed to a man, was considered married, it was a legal and binding contract. One would be required to file for a divorce and obtain a "get" (divorce papers), even in the betrothal stage in order to be free of each other. The wife was the husband's possession of a special sort, and adultery constituted a violation of the husbands exclusive right to her.

- Adultery is prohibited in the Ten Commandments. *(Exodus 20:13; Deuteronomy 5:18)*

- Like all sexual wrongs, it defiles those who commit it. *(Leviticus 18:20; Numbers 5:13; Proverbs 6:32)*

- It is termed the great sin in Genesis 20:3-9.

- The prohibition of adultery is of Divine origin, God, as well as the husband is offended by adultery. *(Genesis 20:6; 39:8-9)*

So, if as supposed by traditional Christianity that Yeshua had no human birth father, then in the same breath wouldn't they also be claiming that God had impregnated another man's wife?

Now no one is suggesting that God had a sexual relation with Mary, but rather that traditional Christianity believes that God had miraculous impregnated Mary.

Nonetheless, it would still constitute impregnating another man's wife, a form of adultery.

Therefore, it is absurd to think that God had impregnated another man's wife! Why would God do that which He Himself considers detestable? He wouldn't!

The problem lies within the English translations that of being far removed from the Biblical Hebraic mindset, therein translating the text with a preconceived mentality.

Let's take a closer look at Matthew 1:18, first we'll look at two English translations of the Greek text, and then compare them with a literal English translation of the Greek text.

NKJV Matthew 1:18

> Now the birth of Jesus Christ was as follows: After His mother Mary was betrothed to Joseph, before they came together, <u>she was found with child</u> of the Holy Spirit.

NASB Matthew 1:18

> Now the birth of Jesus Christ was as follows: when His mother Mary had been betrothed to Joseph, before they came together <u>she was found to be with child</u> by the Holy Spirit.

From the above two verses, the words underlined will be our subject of discussion.

Where many English translators have "<u>she</u> <u>was</u> <u>found</u>," the Greek word (αὐτοὺς - autous) here is NOT a feminine pronoun, but rather it is a masculine pronoun, therefore the text should read "he" not "she."

Also, the English words "was" and "with child" is NOT in any Greek text, they are supplied words by English translators.

Additionally, the Greek word for "found," refers to; "found out, learned or discovered" something.

Since the word is "he" and not "she," as well as, "with child" not being in the Greek text, it then becomes quite obvious that the English translators reading: "<u>she was found with child</u>," is a complete English fabrication of the Greek text of Matthew 1:18.

The mere fact that the masculine pronoun being a "he" referring to Joseph, and his genealogy (Matthew 1:16-17), proves that English translators supplied the words "with child," as no one in their right mind would claim that; "<u>he</u> <u>was</u> found to be <u>with child</u>." So English translators not only having supplied the words "with child," but also changed the masculine pronoun to a feminine pronoun. A lot of manipulation went into their scheme in order to keep their Mystery Babylon religion alive.

So it was Joseph that had "learned something," not Mary, this is confirmed in the very next verse of Matthew 1:19, that caused Joseph to contemplate a resolution to what he had just learned. More on this subject momentarily.

Additionally, why would Mary have the need to learn or discover "the something?" Doesn't Mary already know "the something" as indicated by the message already given to her firsthand by the angel of the LORD in Luke 1:31-33; <u>that she will conceive</u> (future tense) (συλλήμψῃ - sullempse, root word is: συλλαμβάνω - sullambano) <u>in womb</u> (γαστρὶ - root word is: γαστήρ - gastri) <u>and give birth to the Messiah</u>?

Luke 1:31-33

> 31- Behold "You will conceive (future tense) in your womb
> and give birth (future tense) to a son, and you are to call
> (future tense) his name Yeshua."
> 32- He will be great/mighty and called son of the Most High,
> and HASHEM, God, will give him (Yeshua) the throne of
> David his (fore-) father, (through "Joseph of the house of
> David" as identified in Luke 1:27);
> 33- and he (Yeshua) will rule the house of Jacob forever /
> eternity, there will be no end to his kingdom.

So why would Mary have need to discover something that she
already knew?

Let's now look at a literal English translation of
Matthew 1:18

> Now the birth of Yeshua the Messiah happened this way.
> Betrothed his mother Mary to Joseph, before their coming
> together (consummating the marriage), **he** found out/learned
> (that) in womb/in conception to have/having of the Holy
> Spirit. (i.e. - God blessing the fruit of her womb, Mary was
> chosen to be the mother of the King, indeed the very
> Messiah).

Since Mary was the one that had a conversation with
the angel of the LORD, who else, other than Mary would be
telling "the something" to Joseph, and that something was
that she would become (future tense) the mother of the King
of the Jews. Mary told Joseph the very thing that the angel had
told her in Luke 1:31-33.
So, what Joseph had learned, from Mary, was that Mary was
blessed, that she was chosen to be the mother of the King of
the Jews.

Upon Joseph's learning or discovering "the something," Mary being favored among women, and blessed is the fruit of her womb, Luke 1:28; 42," Joseph's reaction, his contemplation of what to do next (vs.19) was befitting of a righteous and humble man.

Let's now examine two Scriptures from the NKJV and NASB English translations.

NKJV Matthew 1:19
> Then Joseph her husband, being a just *man,* and not wanting to make her a public example, was minded to put her away secretly.

NASB Matthew 1:19
> And Joseph her husband, being a righteous man and not wanting to disgrace her, planned to send her away secretly.

First off, the words from the NKJV "put her away" or from the NASB "send her away" are inadequate English words to describe the content of Matthew 1:19.
The Greek word (ἀπολῦσαι - apolusai) is better translated as "release or divorce," here in context, release/divorce her from the marriage contract. Therein a literal English translation would read as followed:

Matthew 1:19
> *Now Joseph her husband was righteous and not willing to disgrace her, resolved secretly to release/divorce her (release her from the marriage contract).*

Secondly, the text emphatically states that Joseph was righteous, which meant that he was a Torah observant Jew, in short, Joseph did what was right in the eyes of God.

Now, if as supposed by traditional Christianity that Mary was actually pregnant at this juncture; the right thing for a Torah observant Jew to do when discovering something morally improper, such as his betrothed wife being pregnant and he not being the father, the husband would have been required by God's Torah to bring the offense (adultery) to the High priest for the court to investigate the matter, and then proceed according to God's Torah.

If the wife is found to be pregnant and that the husband is not the father, the Torah requires the adulterous to be stoned to death. *(Leviticus 20:10; Deuteronomy 22:22)*

Stoning by the public, a procedure often prescribed for crimes felt to threaten the wellbeing of the nation as a whole, among which were sexual crimes.

(Leviticus 18:24-27; 20:22; Deuteronomy 24:4; Deuteronomy 22:24; Jeremiah 3:1-2; Ezekiel 16:40; 23:46-47)

If, as supposed by traditional Christianity that Mary was actually pregnant and her husband Joseph not the father of her child, the question begging for an answer is: would a righteous man disobey God's Torah?

If so, then he wouldn't be considered righteous. A person does not become righteous by disobeying God's commandments. It becomes apparent that Matthew intentionally made known Joseph's good character as being a righteous man for a reason.

So, if as supposed by traditional Christianity that Mary is pregnant, then they would also have to claim that Joseph, a righteous man, was double minded, as he sought to not disgrace her and then proceeds to disgrace her by divorcing her when pregnant. To say that Joseph wanted to protect Mary's integrity when "she was found pregnant" outside of one's marriage, is to flat out disregard God's Torah.

The very thought of Mary being pregnant prior to her and Joseph consummating their marriage, simply makes no sense in context with what the whole of Scripture states and commands.

So it is an obvious misnomer that the righteous Joseph had sought to divorce Mary when pregnant, all the while secretly protecting her integrity, is just simply fallacious.

As stated earlier the English word "child" is not found in the Greek text of Matthew 1:18, it is a supplied word by English translators.

The Greek word in the text is (γαστρὶ - gastri), and the Greek dictionary translates this word into English as: womb or stomach.

Depending on the context of Matthew 1:18 along with the surrounding verses, it becomes quite apparent that the word "womb" would apply here and not "stomach." It also becomes apparent that when referring to the "womb," it stands to reason that it will have something to do with conception, or even that of barrenness.

In Matthew 1:18 the Greek word (γαστρὶ - gastri) "in womb/in conception," has been assumed and gravely exaggerated by English translators when they claim that Mary is with child. This fallacy is based upon English translators preconceived assumption and their complete disregard of the masculine pronoun that is factually in the Greek text that it was: "he that had found out/learned that in womb/in conception to have/having of the Holy Spirit." In other words, it was Joseph who had learned (from Mary) that the Holy Spirit, the power, the will of God blessing the fruit of her womb, ensuring conception would occur on their wedding bed.

Also what is factually in the Greek text, and is followed after the word "in womb/in conception" is: "to have/having of the Holy Spirit."

What does it mean "to have/having of the Holy Spirit?" Everyone coming to faith in the work done at the cross has been given the promise "to have of the Holy Spirit."
(John 7:37-39, Acts 2:38-39; 8:14-17; 19:1-7)
No one in their right mind would ever infer that "to have of the Holy Spirit" to mean God impregnated them!
Every believer emphatically understands that "to have of the Holy Spirit" refers to "being blessed" in some way. This is the exact same understanding in Mary's case, God has opened Mary's womb, making her fertile, not impregnating her in some unconventional way.

Just as, God had blessed Sarah and Elisabeth in opening their womb, making them fertile in their old age.
Rachel too was barren and God blessed the fruit of her womb, opening her womb, making her fertile, not impregnating her or any other woman.
(Genesis 11:30; 17:16-17, 19, 21, 18:10-14, 29:31; 30:1-2, 22-24; 49:25, Deuteronomy 7:13; Judges 13:2-3, 5, 7, Psalms 127:3, Luke 1:7, 13-16, 18, 24-25, 41-42)

Genesis 17:16
> *I (HASHEM, God), will bless her (Sarah); indeed, I will give you (Abraham) a son through her; I will bless her and she will give rise to nations; kings/rulers of peoples will rise from her.*

There is absolutely nothing in the Greek text that indicates that Mary is pregnant prior to her and Joseph coming together. The text states only that "in womb/in conception to have/having of the Holy Spirit." In other words, God is blessing the fruit of her womb: opening the womb, enabling fertility for her to receive Joseph's seed (descendant of David) when the time is to arrive.

If, as supposed by traditional Christianity, that God had actually impregnated Mary (another mans wife), her husband Joseph would then have the perfect defense for convicting God of adultery, God would have no recourse or defense! Do you see how absurd this is? Again, this is worth repeating, the prohibition of adultery is of Divine origin, God as well as the husband is offended by adultery. *(Genesis 20:6; 39:8-9)*.

Therefore, it is preposterous to think that God had impregnated another man's wife! God would not do something that He Himself considers detestable.

Therefore, "in womb/in conception to have/having of the Holy Spirit" the only thing discovered, or found out here, by Joseph, is that Mary is blessed to be the future mother of the long awaited King of the Jews.

The text does not say nor imply that the Holy Spirit impregnated Mary, the text, merely states that "in womb/ in conception to have/having of the Holy Spirit," i.e. - God's blessing.

The power, the will of God is orchestrating, through Mary and Joseph, the very conception and birth of the Messiah to come into the world at this precise hour in history, in order to save His people from their sins.

In other words, God is opening Mary's womb to receive Joseph's seed, not impregnating another man's wife.

God has chosen and blessed not only Mary, but also Joseph, a righteous man and a descendant of David the king. God has sanctified their union: "Joseph, the husband of Mary, out of it (their union) was born Yeshua, called the Messiah." *Matthew 1:16*

Carpenter's Son

Matthew 1:20 ½
> *The angel of the LORD tells Joseph: "do not fear to take Mary your wife."*

From this verse we discover that Joseph had a healthy dose of fear come over him after he had learned from Mary that: "in womb/in conception to have/having of the Holy Spirit." (God blessing the fruit of her womb, Mary is blessed to be the future mother of the long awaited King of the Jews, *Luke 1:26-38).* Fear being the driving force behind Joseph's resolve to release Mary from their marriage contract, all the while having great respect for Mary, as he was concerned for her integrity "not willing to disgrace her."

Matthew 1:19
> *Now Joseph her husband was righteous and not willing to disgrace her, resolved secretly to release/divorce her.*

What was Joseph's mindset that had caused fear to come over him, and why did he think that he would be disgracing Mary, if he had remained married to her?

It can't be said with any certainty of specificity as to why Joseph was afraid to take Mary his wife, as Scripture is vague on Joseph's reasoning. However, there are several facts that do hint to a plausible explanation. Factually, we know that:

1- Joseph was righteous, which embodies humility. *(Matthew 1:19)*
2- Joseph was a carpenter. *(Matthew 13:55)*

3- After the fact, we learn that: Joseph and Mary were relatively poor. *(Luke 2:24)*

Luke 2:24 sheds light on Joseph and Mary's financial situation:

And to offer a sacrifice of a pair of doves or two young pigeons, as required by the Torah of HASHEM.

Which comes from the book of *Leviticus 12:8*

If she can't afford a lamb, then she is to take two doves or two young pigeons, one for a burnt offering and one for a sin offering; and the priest will make atonement for her, and she will be clean.

The fact that Joseph and Mary were unable to offer a lamb for Mary's purification is a great tell that they were relatively poor.

Joseph certainly wasn't living the status quo of a descendant of King David living in a king's palace with all the pomp and fan fare. Joseph wasn't living a life style of the ruling class, not that of a prince or that of a noble, he was outside the aristocratic circles. Joseph was a carpenter, he, like most moderns, living paycheck to paycheck per se.

Joseph having just learned of Mary's status "to be the mother of the King of the Jews" *(Matthew 1:18 Luke 1:31-33)*, was Joseph, now contemplating the particulars of raising and supporting the King of the Jews with his status quo on a carpenters wage?
Did Joseph now think that he would be disgracing Mary if he continued forward with the marriage contract in consideration of his lowly status quo?

All to often the righteous do not recognize their self worth, did Joseph feel unworthy of such an extraordinary blessing, and thereby resolve to release Mary, enabling her to marry another from the tribe of Judah that had prominence?

No doubt that Joseph believed that Mary would be the mother of the future King, but what Joseph didn't realize at this hour, that he too had been chosen to be the father of the future King, and had possibly thought that another man, a man of prominence could just as easily fill those shoes.
At this point, for Joseph it wasn't a question of who the father would be, other than being a direct descendant of king David, through Solomon, et al, for their were many descendants, it was a matter of Joseph's belief that Mary would be the mother of the future King.
Joseph possibly thought that with his seemingly lowly status quo, according to worldly standards anyway, that it would be humiliating for Mary and the future King to live in such a lowly state.

The above consideration is enough to cause any man of humility to gain a healthy dose of fear.
If this is what Joseph was considering, he certainly was not alone in his thoughts.

Take for instance the Scriptures of Matthew 13:54-58 *(Mark 6:1-6 parallel Scriptures).*

Matthew 13:54-58
> *Having come into his hometown, he (Yeshua) taught them in their synagogue, so that they were astounded, and said, where does his wisdom and miracles come from?*
> *Isn't he the carpenter's son? Isn't his mother's name Mary and his brothers Jacob, Joseph, Simon and Judah? Also his sister's, aren't they all with us? So where does he get all this? And they took offense at him.*

But Yeshua said to them, "A prophet is not respected in his hometown and in his own house." And he did few miracles there because of their lack of trust.

They questioned where Yeshua's wisdom and miracles had come from, and then proceeded with questions they fully knew the answers to. It was if to say, a carpenter's son, a country bumpkin, a person of lowly status quo, he couldn't possibly amount to much, certainly not ascend the throne of king David, let alone be the Messiah!
They were expecting pomp and fan fare in the midst of wisdom and miracles, the people ignored reality in exchange for their preconceived expectation of the status quo, anything short of their expectation, they were offended.

Even the wise men (magi) had expected the King of the Jews to be born in a king's palace in Jerusalem with all the pomp and fan fare, as that was the first place the wise men had gone in search of the newborn King of the Jews. *(Matthew 2:1-12)*

However, humankind thinks, and God laughs. All too often God called the humble and the lowly for just the right job, Joseph's humility fit God's bill perfectly, it doesn't fit the world's standards, but it certainly fit God's standards, and that's what counts!

Joseph Took His Wife

Taking a look now at two popular Bible translations of the book of Matthew, chapter one, verses 20, 24 and 25.

NKJV Matthew 1:20, 24-25

> 20- But while he thought about these things, behold, an angel of the Lord appeared to him in a dream, saying, "Joseph, son of David, do not be afraid to <u>take</u> to you Mary your wife, <u>for that which is conceived in</u> her is of the Holy Spirit.
>
> 24- Then Joseph, being aroused from sleep, did as the angel of the Lord commanded him and <u>took</u> to him his wife,
>
> 25- and did <u>not know her</u> till she had brought forth her <u>firstborn</u> Son. And <u>he</u> called His name JESUS.

NASB Matthew 1:20, 24-25

> 20- But when he had considered this, behold, an angel of the Lord appeared to him in a dream, saying, "Joseph, son of David, do not be afraid to <u>take</u> Mary as your wife; <u>for the Child who has been conceived in</u> her is of the Holy Spirit.
>
> 24- And Joseph awoke from his sleep and did as the angel of the Lord commanded him, and <u>took</u> *Mary* as his wife,
>
> 25- but <u>kept her a virgin</u> until she gave birth to a Son; and <u>he</u> called His name Jesus.

Again, after reading these or any English translation of the above verses, it isn't surprising as to why traditional Christians believe what they do; that being that "Mary had conceived prior to her and Joseph's coming together."

However, upon closer examination, the Greek text once again will tell a very different story.

First off, the NASB has supplied the words "child" (vs.20) and "kept virgin" (vs.25), neither of which are in the Greek text.

Now a literal translation:

Matthew 1:20½
> While Joseph was considering this: (vs. 19 releasing Mary
> from the marriage contract) when the angel of the LORD
> appeared to him in a dream and said, "Joseph son of David do
> not fear to take Mary your wife."

This statement by the angel of the LORD is three-fold:

1- "Joseph son of David"
This factual statement by the angel of the LORD
is purposeful and a stark reminder to Joseph,
that as a son of David, his lineage qualifies his
descendant to sit on the throne of David as King.

2- "Mary your wife"
Having foreknowledge we know that Mary has
been chosen to be the mother of the future King.
It is here that the angel of the LORD bids Joseph
to not fear to take Mary his wife, therein, Joseph,
as Mary's husband and descendant of David,
herein, it stands to reason then that Joseph too
has been chosen to be the father of the future
King.

3- "To Take"
Here in context refers to sexual content,
"consummating the marriage."

"To Take (vs.20)" and "Took (vs.24)" - The Greek word:
(παραλαβεῖν - paralabein, παρέλαβεν - parelaben, the root
word for both words, is: παραλαμβάνω - paralambano) of
which the Greek dictionary translates to English as:

To take possession of; to seize, capture; to take with one. Near, beside, along/to take, seize, to receive, take in.

Of course context is vital in understanding content. Here, both Matthew 1:20 "take" and Matthew 1:24 "took" both refer to sexual content.
The Hebraic concept of the act of marriage is simply called "taking" when a man takes a wife. *(Deut. 24:1)*

Exodus 2:1-2
> *There went a man of the house of Levi, and he "took" a daughter of Levi, the woman conceived and gave birth to a son.*

This is the exact same concept with Joseph; he "took" his wife (consummated the marriage).

Now, the last section of Matthew 1:20

> *"… because this with her to beget/to father, is of the Holy Spirit"* (God blessing their union).

The angel of the LORD then continues, but now goes on to explain to Joseph why he shouldn't fear to take Mary his wife, *"Because this"* (the taking of his wife) *"with her"* (both Mary and Joseph where conception begins) *"to beget"* (of men begetting children, but by extension of the mother) this begetting *"is of the Holy Spirit."* (God blessing their union.) Verse 20 confirms what verse 18 has already stated "in womb/in conception to have/having of the Holy Spirit." In short, the opening of Mary's womb to receive Joseph's seed: fertility, ensuring conception. God is blessing their union, ensuring that His anointed one (the Messiah) will come forth.

What would the point be for the angel of the LORD to meticulously articulate, that:

1- Joseph is a son of David.

2- Bidding Joseph to not fear to take Mary his wife.

If in the end Joseph has nothing to do with his wife Mary's pregnancy? Has the angel of the LORD nothing better to do than to layout a premise only to confuse and play head games with Joseph? Of course not! The message of the angel of the LORD is articulate and purposeful.

In the Greek text of Matthew 1:20, the Greek word ("γεννηθὲν - gennethen") has been translated by English translators as "conceived" implying that Mary was already pregnant prior to her and Joseph's coming together.
However, if the Greek text wanted to say "conceived" it would have chosen the Greek word ("συνείληφεν - suneilephen") as exampled in Luke 1:36.

Luke 1:36
> *Behold, your relative Elizabeth even she conceived ("συνείληφεν*[37] *- suneilephen") a son in her old age, and this is the sixth month for her who was called barren.*

Two very distinct Greek words: ("γεννηθὲν - gennethen" Matthew 1:20) and ("συνείληφεν - suneilephen" Luke 1:36), and yet, English Bible translators have translated these two distinct Greek words into one common English word.

---

37 Both Greek words of Luke 1:36 ("συνείληφεν - suneilephen") and Luke 2:21 ("συλλημφθῆναι - sullemphthenai") are from the same Greek root word ("συλλαμβάνω - sullambano") to seize, to take, to conceive, to become pregnant.

Now, all the "begets" or "fathered" of Matthew 1:2-16 (ἐγέννησεν - egennesen), including Yeshua in verse 16 (ἐγεννήθη - egennethe), along with Matthew 1:20 our subject (γεννηθὲν - gennethen), the root word for each and every single one of these Greek words is ("γεννάω - gennao").

The Greek dictionary translates the Greek word ("γεννάω - gennao") into English as: to engender, to beget.

The English dictionary defines those archaic words as followed:

> Engender: beget, procreate (of a father) beget (offspring)
>
> Beget:　　to procreate as the father, (he begat a son/he fathered a son)
>
> Properly:　of men begetting children, but by extension of the mother.

The Hebrew equivalent to the Greek word ("γεννάω - gennao") is ("יָלַד - yalad").

The Hebrew dictionary translates the Hebrew word ("יָלַד - yalad") into English as: to bring forth, to bear, to beget, to be born, to procreate.

Now the Greek root word ("γεννάω - gennao") in its variant forms is found in the Newest Testament a total of 97 times[38].

38　The Greek root word ("γεννάω - gennao") is found in its variant forms 97 times in the following Scriptures. Mt. 1:2-16,20; 2:1, 4; 19:12; 26:24; Mk. 14:21; Lk. 1:13, 35, 57; 23:29; John 1:13; 3:3-8; 8:41; 9:2,19-20, 32,34; 16:21; 18:37; Acts 2:8; 7:8,20,29; 13:33; 22:3, 28; 2Pet 2:12; 1John 2:29; 3:9; 4:7; 5:1, 4,18; Rom 9:11; 1Cor 4:15; Gal 4:23-24, 29; Heb 1:5; 5:5; 11:12,23; 2Tim 2:23; Philem 1:10

In 96 out of the 97 times found, English Bible translators have translated this Greek word as:

Begat, begot, begotten, father, fathered, born, borne, bear, bare, bore, brought forth, gave birth.

With the majority word translated as: begat/begot, father and born.

96 out of 97 times English translators were consistent with their understanding and translation of the Greek word ("γεννάω- gennao"). But when approaching Matthew 1:20 they altered the original Greek definition and took great liberties when they supplied the word "conceived."

Let's see how well the word "conceived" fits into Yeshua's genealogy account of Matthew 1:2.

Abraham conceived Isaac,
Isaac conceived Jacob.

Only in the Hollywood fantasy film "Junior" does a man conceive.

To beget or engender, applies to men begetting children, but by extension of the mother: Abraham begat or fathered Isaac, Isaac begat or fathered Jacob.

At Matthew 1:20, 24 and 25 English translators are at odds with their own translation, and yet, translators and readers alike have not raised an eyebrow to these irreconcilable English words.

Using the NKJV for our example, however one can peruse any English Bible version to see the same point of contention.

NKJV - Matthew 1:

> vs. 20 - do not be afraid "to take" to you Mary your wife
>
> vs. 24 - Joseph did as the angel of the LORD commanded him and "took" to him his wife
>
> vs. 25 - and did "not know her"

Take notice of the words "Take" (vs. 20), "Took" (vs. 24), and "Not Know Her" (vs. 25), as well as, bearing in mind our earlier discussion of the Hebraic concept of the act of marriage, is simply called "Taking" when a man takes a wife. *(Deut. 24:1, Ex 2:1-2)*

Now, English translators on the one hand claim that:

> Joseph "Took" his wife (having sexual relation) vs. 24.

Yet, on the other hand they claim that:

> Joseph did "not know her" (not having sexual relation) vs. 25.

Either Joseph had marital relations, or he did not have marital relations with his wife Mary, it is an either or situation!
English translations are confusing at best, and yet readers just move forward never questioning the duplicity of thought.

First, lets clarify the words chosen in verse 25: "not know her," the word "her" here is not in any Greek text, we'll discuss this further momentarily.
Now, as subtle as the words "not know" may appear in verse 25, English translators have again taken a toll on the minds of their readers. Its not that the English words chosen "not know" is incorrect per se, but rather that the English mindset

when translating the Greek text, lacks its underlining Hebraic mindset. Therein, the subtleness of the many English translations of this verse, herein have left the reader with a large dose of conjecture. Or, English translators were making use of cleaver and indirect methods to achieve something other than its original intent.

The Greek word: (ἐγίνωσκεν - eginosken), of which the Greek dictionary translates into English as:
to perceive, gain knowledge (of), to know, learn, understand; to judge, determine, decide; to think; to resolve.

As seen from the definition above, the word "know" here, refers to "knowledge, perception, insight or understanding" of something, it has absolutely nothing to do with sexual content.
In verse 25, to not know, simply refers to not understanding something. This exact same Greek word spelling can be found in Mark 15:10, Luke 7:39, John 2:25.

Therefore, Joseph Took his wife (consummated the marriage vs.24), but did not understand (something vs.25)

Before addressing the "something" that Joseph did not understand at this time, we first need to address other issues in verse 25.

Now, at Matthew 1:25, there are two schools of thought with the Greek word "ου - hou"

1- Novum Testamentum Graece/NA27[39] Greek text: its claimed that the Greek word "ου" is a neuter pronoun, therein the English translation of Matthew 1:25 would read as:

---

39 NA27 – Nestle Aland 27th edition

"but did not understand until she bore
"their" son and called his name Yeshua."

2- W&H[40] Greek text: its claimed that the Greek word
"ου" is a masculine pronoun, therein the English
translation of Matthew 1:25 would read as:

"but did not understand until she bore "his"
son and called his name Yeshua."

Either way, this pronoun is not in the feminine as many
English translators have claimed by their translation, the
general consensus translation: "and did not know her until
she bore her son."

However, the NA27 and W&H Greek text has only one
feminine pronoun (she), not three feminine pronouns.

Now the Byzantine/Majority[41] Greek text is identical with the
NA27 and W&H with the exception of an additional Greek
words "αυτης τον πρωτοτοκον " of which translates to "her
firstborn," therein the English translation of Matthew 1:25
according to the Byzantine text would read as:

"but did not understand until she bore their/his son
"her firstborn" and called his name Yeshua."

Therein the Byzantine text would have two feminine
pronouns do to the additional text, not three feminine
pronouns.

---

40 W&H – Westcott and Hort
41 Byzantine, also called the Majority Text, it also underlies the
Textus Receptus of which the KJV derives.

All English translators have omitted the neuter/masculine pronoun "their/his" and all having supplied a feminine pronoun in its place, which otherwise does not exist.

Additionally, all English translators have supplied an extra masculine pronoun "he" toward the mid-end of the sentence, which does not exist in any of the aforementioned Greek texts.

The general consensus of English translations is:

"and "<u>he</u>" called his name Jesus/Yeshua."

The Greek text does not have an additional masculine pronoun here for "<u>he</u>."

The Greek text simply translates to English as:

"and called his name Yeshua."

The NA27 and W&H text has one feminine pronoun "she" (bore) and one neuter/masculine pronoun "their/his" (son) and one masculine pronoun "his" (name Yeshua).
The Byzantine text has two feminine pronouns "she" (bore) and "her" (firstborn), and one neuter/masculine pronoun "their/his" (son) and one masculine pronoun "his" (name Yeshua).

The Greek texts do not have three feminine pronouns as indicated by English translators. They either have one or two feminine pronouns depending on what Greek text is read, and all having only one neuter/masculine pronoun "their/his" and one masculine pronoun "his."

The Greek pronoun "ου - hou" links verses 24 and 25 together:

> vs. 24- Joseph (our subject) did what the angel of the LORD commanded him, and took his wife (consummated the marriage),
> vs. 25- but (Joseph) did not understand (something) until - she bore their/his son [her firstborn] and called his name Yeshua.

After Mary gave birth and called his name Yeshua, Joseph now understands something that he had not previously understood.

Called His Name Yeshua

Matthew 1:25
> *but did not understand (something vs. 21-23) until she bore their/his son and called his name Yeshua.*

From the structure of this verse, we now know, that it was Mary, not Joseph, who had called his name Yeshua.

Matthew 1:21 also attest that it would be Mary that would call his name Yeshua.

> *And will (future tense) bear a son and call his name Yeshua, for he will save His people from their sins.*

Again, when reading various English translations of this verse, translators have again supplied words such as: "you are" or "you shall" call his name Jesus/Yeshua, implying that it was Joseph who called his name Yeshua. But again, these words are not in the Greek texts.

Very little is said in Scripture with regard to what Mary and Joseph may or may not have conveyed to one another about their individual conversations they had with the angel of the LORD.
But, the fact remains that Joseph did not understand something prior to Mary giving birth and calling his name Yeshua, this tells us that Joseph, after the fact, now understands something more than he previously knew.

Joseph having earlier understood that his son would sit on the throne of David, as King, but it was here, at this very moment, when Mary called his name Yeshua "God's Salvation[42]," that Joseph had an eye-opening revelation moment.

Joseph now understood the totality of the prophecy given him by the angel of the LORD just a few verses back 21 - 23. That Yeshua not only was the newborn King of the Jews, but now Joseph understood that Yeshua was the very Messiah, "the anointed one of God," the very one that would save His people from their sins, the very salvation of humanity would rest on Yeshua's shoulders.

Having now a better understanding of these verses, lets take a fresh look at Matthew 1:20, 24-25 in context, before moving on to the final topic of this chapter.

---

42 Yeshua's Hebrew name means: God's salvation.
Hence, Yeshua is the means of God's salvation for humankind. (*Mt. 1:21*)

Matthew 1:20

> *But while he was considering this (divorce vs.19), an angel of the LORD appeared to him in a dream and said, Behold, "Joseph son of David," do not fear to take Mary your wife (consummate the marriage), because this with her to beget/father, is of the Holy Spirit (God blessing their union).*
>
> *24- Then Joseph rose up from his sleep to do that what the angel of the LORD commanded him and took his wife (consummated the marriage),*
>
> *25- but did not understand (something vs.21-23), until she bore their/his son and called his name Yeshua (God's Salvation).*

The Unveiling

If there were just one verse in the Newest Testament that was so clear and concise, that would refute, once an for all, that Mary was not pregnant prior to her and Joseph's coming together, pre-Joseph's encounter with the angel of the LORD, what might that verse look like and is there even such a verse?

Amazingly enough, there is just such a verse and what's more, English translators have accurately translated it. This lone verse has sat behind the scene, undetected for centuries without English translators and laymen alike, never having considered the ramification that this lone verse would have in countering traditional Christianity's well held belief of Mary being pregnant prior to her and Joseph's coming together. In short, a virgin birth theology.

Here is the lone verse:

Luke 2:21
> *On the eighth day, when it was time for his circumcision, he was given the name Yeshua, which is what the angel had called him before his conception in the womb.*

This verse emphatically proves that Mary was not pregnant before the angel of the LORD had revealed the name Yeshua.

> *"The name Yeshua was given <u>before, prior to,</u> his conception in the womb."*

The angel of the LORD having appeared to both Mary and Joseph, at separate intervals, of which, both Mary and Joseph were given the name Yeshua (*Luke 1:31* and *Matthew 1:21*), the name given before he was conceived in the womb (*Luke 2:21*). Therefore, Mary was not pregnant before the angel of the LORD had revealed the name Yeshua to them.

The angel of the LORD said to Mary:

Luke 1:31
> *Behold, "You will conceive (future tense) in your womb and give birth (future tense) to a son, and <u>you are to call (future tense) his name Yeshua.</u>"*

The angel of the LORD said to Joseph:

Matthew 1:21
> *And (she) will (future tense) bear a son and <u>call his name Yeshua,</u> for he will save His people from their sins.*

With Luke 2:21 now in the forefront of our understanding, it becomes evident that the virgin birth theology is a fallacy, brought to the world at large from the school of thought of Babylon, compliments of the work of Satan in deceiving the masses.

Earlier having demonstrated that English translators mistranslated Matthew 1:18, 20 and 25, and now with Luke 2:21 validating what we have been saying all along; that Mary was not pregnant pre-Joseph's encounter with the angel of the LORD, when the angel had revealed the name Yeshua to Joseph, and that Mary did not become pregnant until Joseph "took" his wife. *(Matthew 1:24)*

By the grace and blessing of God's hand, God ensured through Joseph and Mary conception of His anointed one, the Messiah, the one that would save His people from their sins. HalleluYah! (Praise God)

Chapter Six

<u>Prophecy of Isaiah 7:14 - Matthew 1:23</u>

The first part of this chapter will focus on the Hebrew and Greek language, a necessary component to prove that many English translators have mistranslated a key word in Isaiah 7:14 and Matthew 1:23.

Beginning with the Hebrew language, we will be using three different Hebrew texts (later three Greek texts) for our Bible language comparison.

The Hebrew language Bibles being used here are as followed:

1) The Biblia Hebraica Stuttgartensia (BHS) is an edition of the Masoretic Text of the Hebrew Bible as preserved in the Leningrad Codex.

2) The Modern Hebrew New Testament (MHNT) is of a modern critical edition of the Greek Newest Testament, and uses a contemporary Israeli Hebrew style.

3) The Delitzsch Hebrew New Testament (DHNT) translation is a Hebrew Translation of the Greek New Testament produced by 19th century German scholar Franz Delitzsch.

Lets now examine the Hebrew language of Isaiah 7:14 and Matthew 1:23. For ease of viewing, paying particular attention to the words enlarged, bold and shadowed for letter and word comparison.

Hebrew is read from right to left.

BHS - Isaiah 7:14 ½

הִנֵּה הָעַלְמָה הָרָה וְיֹלֶדֶת בֵּן **וְקָרָאת** שְׁמוֹ עִמָּנוּ אֵל

MHNT Matthew 1:23

הִנֵּה הָעַלְמָה הָרָה וְיֹלֶדֶת בֵּן **וְקָרָאת** שְׁמוֹ עִמָּנוּ אֵל.

DHNT - Matthew 1:23

הִנֵּה הָעַלְמָה הָרָה וְיֹלֶדֶת בֵּן **וְקָרְאוּ** שְׁמוֹ עִמָּנוּאֵל
אֲשֶׁר פֵּרוּשׁוֹ הָאֵל עִמָּנוּ׃

The subject Hebrew word highlighted is "Karat/Karau" they are variants of the same Hebrew root word "קרא - kara" of which, is identical in meaning and content, it means: to call.

Therein the variant Hebrew spelling וְקָרָאת / וְקָראוּ does not in anyway change the meaning of the Scripture.

Nor is this particular word relevant to our main topic, but felt it necessary to point out in order to not confuse anyone when comparing the collective Hebrew text.

Now the following Hebrew text, Delitzsch (DHNT) text adds four additional Hebrew words that the Biblia Hebraica Stuttgartensia (BHS) and the Modern Hebrew New Testament (MHNT) otherwise does not have.

Those last four Hebrew words literally translate from Hebrew to English as: "which is translated, God with us."

BHS - Isaiah 7:14 ½

הִנֵּה הָעַלְמָֹה הָרָה וְיֹלֶדֶת בֵּ֑ן וְקָרָאת שְׁמֹו עִמָּנוּ אֵל

MHNT Matthew 1:23

הִנֵּה הָעַלְמָה הָרָה וְיֹלֶדֶת בֵּן וְקָראת שְׁמֹו עִמָּנוּ אֵל.

DHNT - Matthew 1:23

הִנֵּה הָעַלְמָה הָרָה וְיֹלֶדֶת בֵּן וְקָראוּ שְׁמֹו עִמָּנוּאֵל

אֲשֶׁר פֵּרוּשֹׁו הָאֵל עִמָּנוּ ׃

Those last four Hebrew words from the DHNT are not part of the original Hebrew it is derived from the Newest Testament Greek.

However, it is only conveying what the word "Immanuel" means. Therein, it does not in anyway change the meaning of the Scripture.

Notice the following Hebrew highlighted words, both BHS and MHNT have separated the Hebrew word "Immanu - el עִמָּנוּ אֵל." Whereas, the DHNT has no separation of the word "Immanuel עִמָּנוּאֵל."

BHS - Isaiah 7:14 ½

הִנֵּה הָעַלְמָה הָרָה וְיֹלֶדֶת בֵּן וְקָרָאת שְׁמוֹ **עִמָּנוּ אֵל**

MHNT Matthew 1:23

הִנֵּה הָעַלְמָה הָרָה וְיֹלֶדֶת בֵּן וְקָרָאת שְׁמוֹ **עִמָּנוּ אֵל**

DHNT - Matthew 1:23

הִנֵּה הָעַלְמָה הָרָה וְיֹלֶדֶת בֵּן וְקָרְאוּ שְׁמוֹ **עִמָּנוּאֵל**
אֲשֶׁר פֵּרוּשׁוֹ הָאֵל עִמָּנוּ׃

The word Immanuel or Immanu - el, whether connected or separated, means the exact same thing.

Lets now examine the Greek language of these same passages, again for ease of viewing, paying particular attention to the words enlarged, bold and shadowed for letter and word comparison.

The Greek language Bibles being used here are as followed:

1) The Septuagint (LXX) is an Ancient Greek transla-tion of the Hebrew Bible (Oldest Testament). The translation process was undertaken in stages, begin-ning 3rd century B.C.E. and completed by 132 B.C.E.

2) Novum Testamentum Graece normally refers to the Nestle-Aland editions (NA27 - 27th edition), named after those who led the critical editing work.

3) Byzantine also called Majority Text, is the form found in the largest number of surviving manuscripts of the Newest Testament, though not the oldest, it also underlies the Textus Receptus Greek Text.

Greek is read from left to right

Septuagint - Isaiah 7:14 ½
ἰδοὺ ἡ παρθένος ἐν γαστρὶ ἕξει καὶ τέξεται υἱόν καὶ **καλέσεις** τὸ ὄνομα αὐτοῦ Εμμανουηλ

Novum Testamentum Graece - Matthew 1:23
ἰδοὺ ἡ παρθένος ἐν γαστρὶ ἕξει καὶ τέξεται υἱόν, καὶ **καλέσουσιν** τὸ ὄνομα αὐτοῦ Ἐμμανουήλ, ὅ ἐστιν μεθερμηνευόμενον μεθ᾽ ἡμῶν ὁ θεός.

Byzantine/Majority Text - Matthew 1:23
ιδου η παρθενος εν γαστρι εξει και τεξεται υιον και **καλεσουσιν** το ονομα αυτου εμμανουηλ ο εστιν μεθερμηνευομενον μεθ ημων ο θεος

The subject Greek words highlighted "Kaleseis / Kalesousin / Kalesousi" are variants of the same Greek root word "καλέω - kaleo" of which, is identical in meaning and content, it means: to call.
Therein the variant Greek spelling **καλέσεις** / **καλέσουσιν** / **καλεσουσιν** does not in anyway change the meaning of the Scripture.

Nor is this particular word relevant to our main topic, but felt it necessary to point out in order to not confuse anyone when comparing the collective Greek text.

Now the following Greek texts of Novum Testamentum Graece and the Byzantine/Majority text adds seven additional Greek words that the Septuagint text otherwise does not have, those last seven Greek words literally translate from Greek to English as: "which is translated, God with us."

Septuagint - Isaiah 7:14 ½
ἰδοὺ ἡ παρθένος ἐν γαστρὶ ἕξει καὶ τέξεται υἱόν καὶ καλέσεις τὸ ὄνομα αὐτοῦ Εμμανουηλ

Novum Testamentum Graece - Matthew 1:23
ἰδοὺ ἡ παρθένος ἐν γαστρὶ ἕξει καὶ τέξεται υἱόν, καὶ καλέσουσιν τὸ ὄνομα αὐτοῦ Ἐμμανουήλ, **ὅ ἐστιν μεθερμηνευόμενον μεθ᾽ ἡμῶν ὁ θεός.**

Byzantine/Majority Text - Matthew 1:23
ιδου η παρθενος εν γαστρι εξει και τεξεται υιον και καλεσουσιν το ονομα αυτου εμμανουηλ **ο εστιν μεθερμηνευομενον μεθ ημων ο θεος**

Collectively, the last four Hebrew words and the last seven Greek words of Matthew 1:23 are not part of the Oldest Testament Hebrew or Oldest Testament Septuagint Greek of Isaiah 7:14; even so, it only refers to what the word "Immanuel" means. Therein, it does not in anyway change the meaning of the Scripture.

With that said, we can agree then that Matthew 1:23 is a direct quote taken from Isaiah 7:14. Therein it stands to reason then that a quote would be an exact copy of the original, word for word, thought for thought, of which it has now been shown to be an authentic true copy of the original.

Lets now examine the Hebrew, Greek and English of Isaiah 7:14 along side Matthew 1:23 (where applicable).
For viewing ease and comparison as well as being our main subject of discussion, the collective text will be highlighted in a single or a double outlined box. For example the Hebrew, Greek and English text in a double outlined box will coincide with its collective double outlined box, and the single outlined box will coincide with its collective single outlined box.

Since the Hebrew and Greek text are identical to their collective text only one example of each will be shown.

BHS Isaiah 7:14 ½

הִנֵּה הָ‏‎עַלְמָה‎‏ הָרָה‎ וְיֹלֶדֶת בֵּן וְקָרֵאת שְׁמוֹ עִמָּנוּ אֵל

Novum Testamentum Graece - Matthew 1:23
ἰδοὺ ἡ παρθένος ἐν γαστρὶ ἕξει καὶ τέξεται υἱόν, καὶ καλέσουσιν τὸ ὄνομα αὐτοῦ Ἐμμανουήλ, ὅ ἐστιν μεθερμηνευόμενον μεθ᾽ ἡμῶν ὁ θεός.

Now, lets take a look at various English Bible translations of the same text of Isaiah 7:14 and Matthew 1:23.

NKJV[43]-Is. 7:14,   Therefore the Lord Himself will give you a sign: Behold, the ⟦virgin⟧ ⟦shall conceive⟧ and bear a Son, and shall call His name Immanuel.

Mt. 1:23,   Behold, the ⟦virgin⟧ ⟦shall be with child,⟧ and bear a Son, and they shall call His name Immanuel," which is translated, "God with us."

ASV[44] - Is. 7:14,   Therefore the Lord himself will give you a sign: behold, a ⟦virgin⟧ ⟦shall conceive⟧, and bear a son, and shall call his name Immanuel.

Mt. 1:23,   Behold, the ⟦virgin⟧ ⟦shall be with child⟧, and shall bring forth a son, And they shall call his name Immanuel; which is, being interpreted, God with us.

NASB[45]- Is. 7:14,   Therefore the Lord Himself will give you a sign: Behold, a ⟦virgin⟧ ⟦will be with child⟧ and bear a son, and she will call His name Immanuel.

Mt. 1:23,   "Behold, the ⟦virgin⟧ ⟦shall be with child⟧ and shall bear a Son, and they shall call His name Immanuel," which translated means, "God with us."

---

43 New King James Version (NKJV)
44 American Standard Version (ASV)
45 New American Standard Bible (NASB)

CJB[46] - Is. 7:14,   Therefore *Adonai* himself will give you people a sign: the young woman will become pregnant, bear a son and name him 'Immanu El [God is with us].

Mt. 1:23,   "The virgin will conceive and bear a son, and they will call him 'Immanu El." (The name means, "God is with us.")

RSV[47] - Is. 7:14,   Therefore the Lord himself will give you a sign. Behold, a young woman shall conceive and bear a son, and shall call his name Immanu-el.

Mt. 1:23 -   "Behold, a virgin shall conceive and bear a son, and his name shall be called Emmanu'el" (which means, God with us).

NRSV[48]-Is. 7:14,   Therefore the Lord himself will give you a sign. Look, the young woman is with child and shall bear a son, and shall name him Immanuel.

Mt. 1:23,   "Look, the virgin shall conceive and bear a son, and they shall name him Emmanuel," which means, "God is with us."

---

46 Complete Jewish Bible (CJB)
47 Revised Standard Version (RSV)
48 New Revised Standard Version (NRSV)

Brenton[49] -Is. 7:14, Therefore the Lord himself shall give you a sign; behold, a ‖virgin‖ ‖shall conceive‖ in the womb, and shall bring forth a son, and thou shalt call his name Emmanuel.

JPS[50] - Is. 7:14, Assuredly, my Lord will give you a sign of His own accord! Look, the ‖young woman‖ ‖is with child‖ and about to give birth to a son. Let her name him Immanuel.

TNK[51] - Is. 7:14 Therefore, my Lord Himself will give you a sign: Behold, the ‖maiden‖ ‖will become pregnant‖ and bear a son, and she will name him Immanuel.

First off, the text highlighted in a double outlined box is in the "future tense" all but two of these English translators have correctly attributed the text in the future tense "will become, will, will be, shall, shall be."

The NRSV at Isaiah 7:14 translated it in the present tense "is with," but at Matthew 1:23 they translated it in the future tense "shall;" and yet the original languages are identical.

49 Sir Lancelot Charles Lee Brenton (Brenton). English translation of the Greek Septuagint

50 Jewish Publication Society (JPS) English translation of the Hebrew Bible (Oldest Testament).

51 Tanach - Stone Edition (TNK) English translation of the Hebrew Bible (Oldest Testament).

Secondly, having earlier discussed in chapter five, subtitled Joseph's Character, the Greek word γαστρι - gastri, means: womb or conception, and not the word "child" as many English translators like to claim it is at Matthew 1:18, 23. Here in Matthew 1:23 you'll notice that some English translators did translate γαστρι - gastri as conceive, a synonym of the word conception.

Turning our attention now to our second word that is highlighted in a single outlined box. At first glance of the above English Bible versions one would think that the NKJV, ASV and the NASB have accurately translated the Hebrew word הָעַלְמָה (al'mah), and the Greek word παρθένος, (par-then´-os) as "virgin" because they were consistent with their use of the same English word in both Scripture passages of Isaiah 7:14 and Matthew 1:23.

However, let us be diligent and cross-examine these words, where in fact you will see that in this particular instance, the CJB, RSV, NRSV, JPS and the TNK have actually translated correctly the Hebrew word הָעַלְמָה (al'mah) and the Greek word παρθένος (par-then´-os) as "young woman" in Isaiah 7:14, and that all of the above mentioned English versions, where applicable, all having mistranslated Matthew 1:23 as "virgin."

Why all the confusion within the English translations? It certainly has raised a flag of suspicion with the English translators dualism, given the fact that Matthew 1:23 is an exact copy of the original, Isaiah 7:14.

Perhaps when some translators are translating certain words, they have already embraced a certain set of doctrines on a given subject that possibly would blind side one from being objective.

The following partial quote was taken from Wikipedia. org[52]

It reads:

Controversial passages

The word "parthenos" at the time the Greek edition of Isaiah was written only indicates a young woman. The implication of a "virgin" only developed later in Greek language. By the time the Gospel of Matthew was written, contemporary Greek texts carried the added meaning. Nonetheless, to translate an ancient word with a more modern meaning does not meet the criteria for either a literal or a meaning-for-meaning translation. Therefore, at the time of the Septuagint text of Isaiah, "the young woman" is likely a more appropriate translation than "virgin," which has often been used because of a traditional Christian bias.

      With that said, let us continue by first looking up these words in an unbiased Hebrew and Greek language dictionary, followed by theological dictionaries, and finish up by allowing the Scriptures to define its own meaning, giving Scripture the last word.

BHS Isaiah - 7:14½

הִנֵּה הָ‎עַלְמָה‎ הָרָה וְיֹלֶדֶת בֵּן וְקָרָאת שְׁמוֹ עִמָּנוּ אֵל

The Hebrew word highlighted in a single outlined box is: (עַלְמָה - *al'mah*)

---

52 http://en.wikipedia.org/wiki/New_Revised_Standard_
Version. Article has since been removed. Nonetheless, it was worth noting.

Hebrew Language Dictionary

Hebrew - הָעַלְמָה (ha'al'mah) - (the letter הָ (hey) at the beginning of this word is referred to as the definite article), as in "the al'mah."

עַלְמָה (al'mah) - (Feminine form)

  1- young woman, maiden, damsel, marriageable girl, Miss.

  2- maiden, young marriageable woman

This word does not reflect sexual behavior, that of a virgin, or a non-virgin. It simply refers to a young woman, specifically a young woman of marriageable age.

Let us also examine two archaic English words that are part of the Hebrew definition:

  Maiden - A girl, young woman, unmarried woman; maid. (a girl; a female, a young or relatively young woman)

  Damsel - A young unmarried woman.

These Old English words, "maiden and damsel," have no correlation to the woman's sexual behavior.
It does not mean that she has, or has not, been sexually active. The Hebrew dictionary reflects only an age of the female, which would be upward of puberty, the period of sexual maturity and capable of reproduction.

A young widow of sexual maturity and capable of reproduction, could be an עַלְמָה - al'mah, yet, obviously a widow would have had sexual relations with her husband prior to his death, and may have bore him many children. If this widow were still young (capable of reproduction), she would be considered an "עַלְמָה - al'mah," a young unmarried woman.

The masculine equivalent of the feminine "עַלְמָה - al'mah," is "עֶלֶם - elem," its definition is: a youth, young man, which would be upward of puberty, the period of sexual maturity and capable of reproduction.
Therein, feminizing these terms would result in "עַלְמָה - al'mah" being a young woman, which would be upward of puberty, the period of sexual maturity and capable of reproduction.

Whether in the feminine or masculine form, there is no mention as to the young persons sexual behavior. The word only refers to an age capable of reproduction, not to the person's sexual activity.

The Hebrew letter מ (mem) in "עַלְמָה - al'mah" and the Hebrew letter ם (mem) in "עֶלֶם - elem" are the same letter. This closed ם (mem) is in its final form. If there were a Hebrew letter after the closed mem ם, then it would appear as an open mem מ. But since it is the last letter in the word, its form changes to a closed mem ם, there is no difference in meaning.

Note the Hebrew letters in the feminine form "עַלְמָה - al'mah" are the same letters in the masculine form "עֶלֶם - elem," less the letter ה (hey) at the end of the word in the masculine form, by which making the one feminine and the other masculine. So if the masculine form concurs to being a young man, wouldn't the feminine form be a young woman? Yes, of course.

This particular Hebrew masculine word "עלם - elem" is found in the Hebrew Bible only two times; *1Samuel 17:56 and 1Samuel 20:22.*
Let's examine several English Bible versions to see their translation of 1Samuel 17:56.
I've chosen this particular verse because there's no such verse in the Septuagint; therefore all English translators were forced to utilize the Hebrew text alone when translating "עלם - elem" without any bias or influence from the Greek Septuagint.

1Samuel 17:56

KJV[53] - And the king said, Inquire thou whose son the <u>stripling</u> is.

NKJV - So the king said, "Inquire whose son this <u>young man</u> *is.*"

ASV - And the king said, Inquire thou whose son the <u>stripling</u> is.

NASB - The king said, "You inquire whose son the <u>youth</u> is."

CJB - The king said, "Find out whose son this <u>boy</u> is."

---

53 King James Version (KJV).

RSV -	And the king said, "Inquire whose son the <u>stripling</u> is."
NRSV -	The king said, "Inquire whose son the <u>stripling</u> is."
GLT[54]-	And the king said, You ask whose son this <u>young man</u> *is.*
GB[55]-	Then the King sayde, Enquire thou whose sonne this <u>yong man</u> is.
JPS -	"Then find out whose son that <u>young fellow</u> is," the king ordered.
TNK -	So the king instructed him, "You ask whose son this <u>youth</u> is."

Not once did any English translator translate the Hebrew masculine word "עלם - elem" as "virgin."

Yet it is the masculine equivalent of the feminine "עַלְמָה - al'mah," our subject.

Al'mah simply means "young woman" as Elem simply means "young man."

The Hebrew word "עַלְמָה - al'mah" (feminine) is found in the Hebrew Bible seven times:

Genesis 24:43, Ex. 2:8, Isaiah 7:14, Psalms 68:26, Proverbs 30:19, Song 1:3, Song 6:8

---

54 Green's Literal Translation (GLT) by Jay P. Green, Sr.
55 The Geneva Bible (GB)

Yet, the Greek Septuagint gives two different Greek words when translating the one Hebrew word "עַלְמָה - al'mah."

1) At Genesis 24:43 and Isaiah 7:14, the Greek word used is; "παρθένος - par-then'-os"

2) At Exodus 2:8 "νεᾶνις - neanis"
Psalms 68:26 "νεανίδων - neanidon"
Proverbs 30:19 "νεότητι - neoteti"
Song 1:3 and Song 6:8 "νεάνιδες - neanides"

The Greek root word is: "νεος - neos."

The feminine being "νεᾶνις - neanis" -
youthful, young woman, youth.

The masculine being "νεᾶνιας - neanias" -
youthful, young man, youth.

One Hebrew word "עַלְמָה - al'mah" is replaced by two Greek words, "παρθένος - par-then'-os" and "νεος - neos."

Again, raising a red flag.

Hebrew Theology Dictionaries:

עַלְמָה - al'mah

BDB[56] - עַלְמָה n.f. young woman (ripe sexually; maid or newly married); עֶלֶם n.m. young man.

GKC[57] - עַלְמָה a young woman, *maid*; עֶלֶם a young man

HALOT[58] - עַלְמָה a young woman עֶלֶם / עֶלֶם a young man

STRONG[59] - 5959. עַלְמָה - almah, *al-maw'*; feminine of 5958; - damsel, maid, virgin.

5958. עֶלֶם - elem, *eh´-lem*; a lad: young man, stripling.

Strong's Concordance states that the Hebrew word "al'mah" is the feminine of the masculine "elem," and yet, when defining the male, they simple state a "young man," but for the female, they added the word virgin to their definition, whereas the masculine is lacking the word virgin.

Again, raising a red flag.

---

56 Brown-Driver-Briggs (BDB)
57 Gesenisus (GKC)
58 Koehler-Baumgartner Hebrew and Aramaic Lexicon (HALOT)
59 Strong's Exhaustive Concordance of the Bible (STRONG)

Greek Language Dictionary

Novum Testamentum Graece - Matthew 1:23
ἰδοὺ ἡ παρθένος ἐν γαστρὶ ἕξει καὶ τέξεται υἱόν, καὶ καλέσουσιν τὸ ὄνομα αὐτοῦ Ἐμμανουήλ, ὅ ἐστιν μεθερμηνευόμενον μεθ᾽ ἡμῶν ὁ θεός.

The Greek word highlighted in the single outlined box is: (παρθένος - par'then'os).

Greek - παρθένος (par-then'-os) - Maiden, virgin, young woman.

The Greek reflects three possible uses for one Greek word:

1- Maiden - (a girl, young woman, unmarried woman; maid) (a girl; a female, a young or relatively young woman) (young unmarried woman - available for marriage - upward of puberty, the period of sexual maturity and capable of reproduction – generally 12 to 40 years of age)

2- Virgin - (never having sexual relations)

3- Young woman - (could be married, unmarried, or widowed - a general term for any young women – upward of puberty, the period of sexual maturity and capable of reproduction - generally 12 to 40 years of age)

With three possibilities, we will need to dig deeper into the Greek language by looking at some related Greek words in order to have a better understanding as to what παρθένος - par-then'-os) infers.

Greek language Dictionary - related words:

παρθενευω - (par-then-euo) to remain a maiden (to remain unmarried).

παρθενια - (par-then-ia) maidenhead.

παρθενιος, παρθενικος - (par-the-ios, par-then-ikos) Of a maiden, maidenly; <u>son of an unmarried woman</u>. (Of a maiden: a girl; a female, a young or relatively young woman)

Although the woman is unmarried, she obviously is not a virgin, as she has had a son, "<u>son of an unmarried woman."</u>

παρθεν-οπιπης - (par-then - o-pi-peys) one who looks at maidens.

From here, we can safely deduce that the Greek root word is, παρθέ/ν - par-the/n, which would be descriptive of our main word (παρθένος - par-then'-os).
All of the related Greek words here do not specifically reflect that of a "virgin," only that of a young woman, young unmarried woman, a maiden (a girl; a young or relatively young woman), irrespective of one never having been previously married, a single mother, a widow, a virgin or a non-virgin.

The basic meaning is simply that of a young woman, or a young unmarried woman, with no reflection to one's sexual behavior, only that of upward of puberty, the period of sexual maturity and capable of reproduction.

Greek Theology Dictionaries:

παρθένος - par-then'-os

Louw & Nida[60] - παρθένος, ου *f:* a female person beyond puberty but not yet married and a virgin (though in some contexts virginity is not a focal component of meaning) - 'virgin, young woman.'

Interesting that Louw & Nida point out two important facts,

1- A female person <u>beyond puberty</u> but not married.

2- In some contexts <u>virginity is not a focal component of meaning</u>.

STRONG - παρθένος parthenos, *par-then'-os;* of unknown origin; a maiden; by implication, an unmarried daughter: - virgin.

Also interesting, is that Strong's reflects three possible uses for one Greek word.

1- maiden (a girl; a female, a young or relatively young woman)

2- an unmarried daughter

3- virgin

Scripture – The Last Word

Let us now examine Scripture, that of itself, will emphatically clarify what a virgin, young woman, and girl is, Scripture having the final authority!

To save time of duplication when quoting Scripture, I will include the Hebrew word along side the Greek word.
For ease of reference and comparison, again highlighting the words in a single or double outlined box, along with the new words introduced in its collective shadowed or stripped outline boxes, each with a unique outline box reflecting its counter of the Hebrew and Greek words.

Genesis 24:16

The girl (נַעֲרָ na'ara, παρθένος par-then-os) was very beautiful, a virgin (בְּתוּלָה be'tu'lah, παρθένος par-then-os) never having had sexual relations with any man. She went down to the spring, filled her jar and came up.

Genesis 24:43

> *here I stand near the spring of water, and it comes to pass,*
> *that the young woman (*עַלְמָה *al'mah,* παρθένος *par-*
> *then-os) that comes out to draw, to whom I shall say, please*
> *give me a sip of water from your jar to drink,*

Notice from the above Scriptures, that only "**one**" Greek word
(παρθένος par-then-os) has been used to describe "**three**"
different Hebrew words;

"**girl** - נַעַר na'ara,"

"**virgin** - בְּתוּלָה be'tu'lah,"

"**young woman** - עַלְמָה al'mah."

Let's again look into the Hebrew dictionary for definition:

1- נַעַר or נַעֲרָה na'ara - girl, maid, young woman, servant
(A general term used for any
female)

2- בְּתוּלָה be'tu'lah - chaste maiden, virgin (Literally a
virgin never having sexual
relation)

3- עַלְמָה al'mah - young woman, maiden, damsel,
marriageable girl, Miss. young
marriageable woman (Any young
woman, upward of puberty,
capable of reproduction)

It becomes abundantly evident from Genesis 24:16 that the Hebrew word בְּתוּלָה - be'tu'lah, distinctly clarifies what a virgin is; one never having sexual relations with any man.

Whereas, the Hebrew words נַעַר or נַעֲרָה na'ara and עַלְמָה al'mah do not reflect sexual behavior.

Yet, the Greek word used to describe all three distinct Hebrew words is παρθένος par-then-os, so from the Greek text how could one possibly know with any certainty, as to what word to translate Isaiah 7:14, our key text?

It now is quite obvious then that there is traditional Christian bias when translating Isaiah 7:14.
Yet, at Isaiah 7:14 and Matthew 1:23, the Hebrew word used is עַלְמָה al'mah, the exact same word used at Genesis 24:43, a young woman.

The original text at Matthew 1:23 is the exact same original text of that of Isaiah 7:14, it is a direct quote and therefore reads identically;

the **young woman** (עַלְמָה al'mah, παρθένος par-then-os) **will conceive**, (הָרָה hara, ἐν γαστρὶ ἕξει) (future tense).

It **DOES NOT** say the "virgin (בְּתוּלָה be'tu'lah, παρθένος par-then-os) will conceive."

The text only reflects that of an age of the female, which would be upward of puberty, the period of sexual maturity and capable of reproduction. In contrast to that of Sarah who in her old age, conceived Isaac, a woman who was beyond the age of reproduction.

Genesis 24:36; "**after her old age**" - is beyond the age of reproduction, long after Sarah's change of life, Sarah bore Abraham a son (he 100 and she 90 years old). After old age refers to no longer able to reproduce, just the opposite of that of a young age - עַלְמָה al'mah (the age of reproduction).

No doubt that Mary was a virgin on her wedding bed when she and Joseph consummated their marriage and she conceiving at that same moment in time, makes Mary a virgin bride, not a virgin birth narrative.

It becomes quite evident that selective parts of the traditional Christian English translation of the Bible have been manipulated; such is the case narrative of the false teachings of a virgin birth, trinity and Torah-less doctrines.
Is it any wonder then that many persons have come away confused, questioning the very validity of the Bible itself, rather than the poor English translation?
The Bible, in its original language is not where the problem lays; it is in the poor translations, the lack of understanding, lacking the Hebraic underlining mindset and culture.
The consequence of traditional Christian English translation bias of the Greek and/or Hebrew text the end result of that action is nothing short of keeping alive the mystery Babylon religion.

The question begging to be asked, who and what lie behind this mask of separation?
It is none other than the anti-messiah, of which has minions of followers doing his dastardly dark perversion, masked by a pretense, most that follow aren't even aware they are actually doing his bidding.

Its time to wake up, "come out of Babylon" (confusion) and its "mystery religion," and come to the Promised Land, up to Jerusalem, where God has chosen to place His Name.

Micah 5:2 (parallel Scripture see Isaiah 2:3)
> *Many nations will go and say, "Come, let us go up to the mountain of HASHEM, to the house of the God of Jacob, He will teach us of His ways and we will walk in His paths." For out of Zion (Tzion) will go forth Torah, the word of HASHEM from Jerusalem.*

The word of the LORD God comes forth from Jerusalem, not Babylon, or America, etc.!

The Sign

Often many readers, and translators alike, approach the Divine records with a well-established set of assumptions. They are unaware of the fact that much of what they understand about scripture is derived from man-made theology. While readily accepting a large dose of tradition, they claim and believe that the Bible is their sole authority, (*not realizing they have pushed their doctrine into the Bible, rather than allowing the word of God to speak for itself.*[61])

This intense desire to believe something is a powerful emotion to overcome! The traditional Christian translation of Isaiah 7:14 and Matthew 1:23 is one such case in point.

For the church at large to place emphasis on the word virgin or young woman as being some type of a sign, is to simply miss the entire point as to why Matthew brought this single verse of Isaiah 7:14 forward in his contextual discourse. Matthew indeed understood the intended prophecy that would be fulfilled; but for seventeen hundred years traditional Christianity has played havoc with this verse. With the church's reinvention of the wheel, by giving this verse a different meaning from that of its original intent, has in fact caused many a persons to veer off course, leading them into unknown territory and into yet further misconceptions.

Thereby, the church has ineffectually caused this verse to have no practical significance. Instead of unveiling Yeshua the Messiah to the world they in fact have hidden him from the world with their false teachings of a virgin birth, trinity and Torah-less narratives.

---

61 The identity of Mashiach: by Anthony Buzzard (*emphasis mine*).

With all reasonable conscience, how is it possible for the entire world to reap a sign from a women's virginity? The only one that would know if a woman was a virgin or not, would be the woman herself and possibly her husband.

So how is it possible for a woman's virginity to be an outward sign to the world at large, let alone, to generations yet unborn long after the death of Mary?

It isn't even remotely possible to reap a sign from a woman's virginity, therefore we must ask ourselves, what then is the sign and significance of that God given sign, what does God want all humanity to reap from this sign?

Before we can reap in the harvest for the answer, we must first examine in context the Scriptures surrounding Isaiah 7. These verses are multifaceted, therefore it will be necessary to bring to light several thoughts in order to see a whole picture; so that when we do contrast Isaiah 7:14 with Matthew 1:23, we are able to take hold of its contextual intent.

During the time of Ahaz (Achaz), king of Judah, the land of Israel was still a divided monarchy, with the northern kingdom having its own ruling king, known as the kingdom of Israel, or poetically called Ephraim.

This division of the two monarchies happened during the reign of Rehoboam, Solomon's son. (1Kings 11:35-40)

During the reign of Ahaz, the house of David received word that the northern kingdom of Israel and the kingdom of Aram had joined forces and were planning to attack and usurp the kingdom of Judah. Ahaz and the people of Judah trembled in fear of them. (Isaiah 7:2)

God said to Isaiah, tell Ahaz to be calm and still, fear not; Let your heart not grow faint before these two smoldering spent firebrands. (Isaiah 7:4)

The northern kingdom of Israel along with the kingdom of Aram, were conspiring evil against the kingdom of Judah, they intended to lay waste to Judah and cause Judah to cease from being a people.

Isaiah 7:6, tells us their intent, they said: "Let us attack Judah and vex it and annex it to ourselves, and crown the son of Tabeel as king within it" (one of their own puppets, amenable to their plans).

In essence, what these two wicked and idolatrous kingdoms were attempting to do by usurping the kingdom of Judah, was remove Judah's scepter, it was an attempt to make God's word null and void.

Whereas, God had said:
"the scepter will not depart from Judah."
Genesis 49:10

Thus said the LORD God:
"It won't succeed, it won't happen!"
Isaiah 7:7

Isaiah 7:7-8: Aram (Damascus) and Ephraim (northern kingdom of Israel) will not usurp Judah, and in fact, Ephraim will cease to be a people in sixty-five more years.
The very thing that Aram and Ephraim planned to do to Judah is in fact the very thing that will happen to them. God will whistle for the enemies to come (Isaiah 5:26, 7:18), Assyria will invade Aram and the northern kingdom of Israel, taking them into captivity to Assyria.
From the Assyrian invasion, it is here that the northern kingdom of Israel will cease being a people, but will one day come under the banner of Judah, hence the Hebrew word "Yehudi" (Jew), which derives its name from "Yehudah" (Judah).
The northern kingdom of Israel will cease to be a people, in which, allowing the divided monarchy to cease, whereby, eventually reuniting all twelve tribes under one united monarchy, under the banner of Judah, with Yeshua the

Messiah (the anointed one of God) the righteous King and Shepherd, ruling not only the house of Jacob (twelve tribes), but all the nations. His kingdom will be an everlasting kingdom.

It will be on that day that the descendant of Jesse (Messiah Yeshua) who stands as a banner (sign) for the peoples, nations will seek him, and his resting place will be glorious.

(Genesis 49:8-12; Ezekiel 37:15-28; John 10:16; Isaiah 14:1-2, 56:3; 11:10)

Isaiah 7:9, God states, pointing out vividly, that the capital of Ephraim is Samaria – from this, we then can deduce that the capital of Judah is Jerusalem. In other words, Ephraim had no business trying to annex the province of Judah's territory for themselves, let alone encroach upon Judah's statues of leadership of the Davidic dynasty, for whom it was predestined; Yeshua the Messiah.

Ahaz, king of Judah was exhorted to trust in the prophecy given him, he was to trust in God for their very guidance and support in this troublesome time instead of relying on human alliances for his help, and if he did not believe the reality of the prophecy given, it is because he lacked faith.

Isaiah 7:10-13; Encouraging Ahaz to believe the prophecy given (that Judah would not be usurped), availing him the opportunity to turn from his evil ways, Ahaz was afforded a golden opportunity to ask for a proof positive sign that would convince himself of the validity of the prophecy given.

Yet, Ahaz contemptuously refused to ask for a sign, as if to say: I don't believe that HASHEM can supply a sign.

To Ahaz' own peril, and that of many in Judah: HASHEM had humbled Judah because of Ahaz king of

Israel[62] for Ahaz had led Judah to disgrace and betrayed HASHEM. (2 Chronicles 28:19)

Instead of Ahaz trusting God, the Creator and Sustainer of life, Ahaz placed his trust in mankind, the created. Talk about poetic justice, Ahaz seeks out the king of Assyria for his help, the very people God Himself whistles for to attack Aram and the northern kingdom of Israel, along with cleansing the defiant ones of the house of Judah. Ahaz not only ignores the prophecy given him, but also completely ignores all the promises God had made to David and his house. Basically, Ahaz doesn't believe that Judah will not be usurped by the northern kingdom of Israel and Aram, therein aligning himself with Assyria.

---

62 The Hebrew text states: "Ahaz king of Israel," rather than, Ahaz king of Judah. Three plausible thoughts come to mind, but of course there could be more thoughts on this subject, of which I'm unaware.

   1- Unintentional scribal error.
   2- The prophecy given, that in 65 more years the northern kingdom of Israel would cease to be a people, ending the divided monarchy, in which, it is the very beginning to the eventual united monarchy. Had Ahaz not been so stiffed-necked and believed the prophecy given him and turned from his evil ways, Ahaz, instead of his son Hezekiah, would have been the one offering his hand to Ephraim to come up to Jerusalem to join Judah for the Passover festival, under the banner of Judah, the beginning of the uniting of the kingdom. (2 Chr. chapters 29 and 30, specifically 30:1)
   3- Ahaz was behaving just like the kings of Israel, pursuing evil by doing many acts of wickedness and idolatry, rather than stepping up to the plate to be a proper king of Judah, pursuing justice and righteousness in the land. Therefore, it isn't without reason as to why the text calls Ahaz: king of Israel.

Ahaz also paid tribute of himself to the king of Assyria, by telling the king of Assyria "I am your servant and your son!"
Shouldn't the kings of Judah be a servant and son of the living God? *(2 Kings 16:7-17; 2Chronicles 28:16-24)*

Just when you think it couldn't possibly get any worse, it does, Ahaz even set his sons a flame, following after the pagan idolatrous practice of other nations *(2Chronicles 28:1-5)*, which of course is forbidden by HASHEM, God, *(Deuteronomy 18:10)*. If it were up to Ahaz, even his son Hezekiah might not have survived!
Thank God, that God is in charge and that God is with us (Immanuel), directing the course of His will, because the righteous Hezekiah was chosen by God to be king of Judah, and was called "ruler of My people." *(2 Kings 20:5)* Hezekiah ate the fat of the land (things went well for him) as soon as he knew to abhor evil and choose good. *(Isaiah 7:15)*

Even though Ahaz had contemptuously refused to ask for a sign, God gave him a sign anyway.
The purpose for giving Ahaz a sign is because he was king of Judah at this time, in which, the kings of Judah were to lead the people to righteousness, toward God's calling and will. God in His mercy was affording Ahaz an opportunity to change from his evil ways.

Being now equipped with some background knowledge of Isaiah 7, we are now ready to address verse 14 for the specific set sign that will launch a series of events.

Isaiah 7:14

> *Therefore, the LORD Himself will give you a sign:*
> *Behold, the young woman will conceive and bear a son and call his name Immanuel (God with us).*

The God given sign for the specific sequence of events to begin unfolding, is a son, an heir to the throne of David, here in context of Isaiah 7, the son born is Hezekiah. The sign is the son, not the woman's virginity.

With the birth of Hezekiah, the prophecy begins unfolding, verse 16 tells us that before this son (Hezekiah) knows to abhor evil and choose good, the land of the two kings whom Ahaz fears, will be abandoned.
With Hezekiah's birth, it triggered the abandonment of the land of the two kings, Aram and Ephraim, those that were attempting to usurp and remove the scepter from the kingdom of Judah.

In addition, in sixty-five years from the time of this prophecy, the northern kingdom of Israel would cease being a people, ending the divided monarchy. (By ending the divided monarchy, a door has been opened for a future united monarchy).

The sign of this son's birth (Hezekiah), it began a specific sequence of events, troublesome times for all of Israel, and that of Judah, although they too would go through a cleansing themselves, a remnant will remain and that remnant will not be taken into Assyrian captivity, nor will the scepter depart from Judah.
Isaiah 7:17; HASHEM will bring upon you (house of Judah) and upon your people and upon your father's family days such as have not come since the day Ephraim (northern kingdom of Israel) turned away from Judah (division of the monarchy): The king of Assyria's invasion.
In other words, God will also cleanse the defiant ones of the house of Judah who had also practiced idolatry as Ephraim had done.
The defiant ones of Judah will also go into captivity along side the northern kingdom of Israel, but a remnant of Judah, those faithful and trusting in God, this remnant will remain.

Isaiah 8:11-16; tells us that those who trust in God and sanctify His Name are to fasten the warning and seal the teaching on the hearts of His students.

So when Ahaz' wife, "the young woman conceives, gives birth to a son (Hezekiah)," Ahaz is to know that God is with them (Immanuel), with Judah. That Judah will not be usurped of its royal scepter, that the land of the two kings (Aram and Ephraim) will be abandoned and that in sixty-five years from the time of this prophecy, Ephraim will cease to be a people, ending the divided monarchy.

The sign is not the young woman's virginity, nor the woman herself, but rather, the son is the sign that signals specific upcoming events.

Even though hard times are at hand, those that sanctify God's name, are to hold fast, knowing that God is with them "Immanuel," that God has not abandoned His people.

Immanuel

Isaiah 7:14½
> *The young woman will conceive[63] and bear a son and call his name Immanuel.*

The Hebrew word Immanuel is not referring to a literal naming of the child, we know that the child Hezekiah was not literally named Immanuel, but rather he was named Hezekiah.

In context of Isaiah 7 "call his name Immanuel" thus in effect prophesying that when this child Hezekiah is born, the people are to know that "God is with them." That God has not abandoned them and that God is fulfilling His promise to David and his house that assuredly the scepter will not depart from Judah.

Now while Hezekiah is still relatively young (Isaiah 7:16 before Hezekiah knows to abhor evil and choose good), it is the land of these two kings: Aram (Damascus) and Ephraim (northern kingdom of Israel) of whom Ahaz fears, their lands will in fact be abandoned.

---

63 The young woman "will conceive" is in the future tense. Now if all of this has come about in order to fulfill the prophecy, what is the point of the prophecy being stated in a future tense at Matthew 1:23: "will conceive?" If Mary was already pregnant as assumed by traditional Christians, then shouldn't the prophecy then read at Matthew 1:22: Now all this came about in order to fulfill what the LORD had said through the prophet (applying the prophecy in a now current event to read as); Mt. 1:23 the young woman "has" conceived and (will) bear a son! But it doesn't say that, both Isaiah 7:14 and Matthew 1:23 are in the future tense " will conceive." The young woman "will conceive" and bear a son and call his name Immanuel.

Hence, Judah will not be abandoned because:

God is with them, watching over them.

Now with regards to the naming of Hezekiah, likewise, we see from Matthew 1:23 being a direct quote of Isaiah 7:14, but here it is in regards to Yeshua.

Matthew 1:23
> Behold *"the young woman will (future tense) conceive and bear a son and call his name Immanuel." (which is translated "God with us.")*

It is now in regards to the naming of Yeshua. We see from Matthew 1:21 and Luke 1:31, at separate intervals, that both Joseph and Mary were told by the angel of the LORD to name him Yeshua.

Matthew 1:21
> *and will bear a son and call his name Yeshua, for he will save His people from their sins.*

Luke 1:31
> *"You will conceive[64] in your womb and give birth to a son, and you are to call his name Yeshua."*

They literally named Yeshua, Yeshua, not Immanuel!
Just as Hezekiah was named Hezekiah, not Immanuel!

---

64 Future tense

Matthew 1:21 not only reveals Yeshua's name, but reveals the very purpose of this son's birth:

"he will save His people from their sins."

Matthew then bringing Isaiah 7:14 forward in his discourse:

Matthew 1:22-23

> 22- *Now all this came about in order to fulfill what the LORD had said through the prophet,*
>
> 23- *"the young woman will conceive and bear a son and call his name Immanuel." (which is translated "God with us.")*

Likewise, the Hebrew word Immanuel is not referring to a literal naming of the child, we know that the child Yeshua was not literally named Immanuel, but rather he was named Yeshua.

The birth of this son, the scion (Isaiah 11 - "a righteous branch will emerge from Jesse," the Davidic lineage of the Messiah), thus in effect prophesying that when this child Yeshua is born, the people are to know that "God is with them," that God has not abandoned them.
It is with this son Yeshua, the scion of the tribe of Judah that God in fulfillment of His promise to David and his house is in fact achieving the intended objective for whom the scepter belongs.

For traditional Christianity to claim as they do that somehow Yeshua is literally Immanuel "God with us," God in the flesh, is simply taking this Scripture verse out of context.

If, as supposed by traditional Christianity that Yeshua is literally Immanuel, God in the flesh, then one would also have to claim that Hezekiah is also literally Immanuel, God in the flesh, this too is of course equally ludicrous.

Additionally, Isaiah 8:8 God calls the land of Israel, Immanuel, does this now mean that the land of Israel is also God? This too is absurd.

The Hebrew word Immanuel is not some type of a mystery code word. The Hebrew word Immanuel is found only at *Isaiah 7:14, 8:8, 8:10 and Matthew 1:23*, it is never used as a proper name, but rather as a statement to the effect that "God is with us, God has not abandoned His people." It does not refer to God in the flesh, or God has come down in the form of a human being, but rather, that God is with us, watching over us, directing the course of His will through history. God is mindful of His promise made to His servant David, namely, securing the throne of David for His anointed one "Messiah Yeshua" God's salvation, this son, the scion of the tribe of Judah will save His people from their sins (redemption of sins).

Through Yeshua the Messiah, the anointed one of God, we have salvation, which restores our relationship with God our Father.

In context of Isaiah 7, the twelve tribes were divided into two divisive kingdoms, it is through this abandonment of the land of the northern kingdom of Israel, that these ten tribes would cease being a people, ending the divided kingdom.

In context of Matthew 1:23 of which, enabling the ten tribes to eventually be grafted back in under the banner of Judah, as one cohesive unified kingdom, under the leadership and righteous rule of Messiah Yeshua, King of kings and Lord of lords.[65] *(Revelation 17:14)*

Not only will Israel be grafted back in, but the nations will also be grafted into the common wealth of Israel. *(Romans 11; John 10:16; Isaiah 14:1, 56:3)*

---

65 Revelation 17:14 speaks of Yeshua (יְשׁוּעַ) as being: "Lord of lords and King of kings." This scripture should be compared along side of Deuteronomy 10:17 "For HASHEM (יְהוָה) your GOD is GOD of gods and LORD of lords."

It is paramount to note that Revelation 17:14 does not say that Yeshua is God of gods! The text of Revelation states only that Yeshua is: "Lord of lords and King of kings," indicating his title of Messiahship (the anointed one OF God).

On the other hand, Deut 10:17 unequivocally states "HASHEM alone is GOD of gods and LORD of lords," indicating His title of Supreme Sovereignty. HASHEM alone is God and there is no other God besides HASHEM. (Deut. 4:16; 5:7)

Unbeknownst to traditional Christianity / Messianic, Yeshua never claimed to be God, or God in the flesh. But what Yeshua did claim, was that he is the Messiah (the anointed one OF God). Immediately after Yeshua was resurrected, Yeshua stated unequivocally that: I am going back to my Father and your Father, to my God and your God (John 20:17). In short, Yeshua recognized that God is his God; therefore, Yeshua is not God!

For more information on the non-trinity, there are two excellent books:

1- The identity of Mashiach (Messiah), a plea for a return to belief in Yeshua, the Mashiach, by Anthony Buzzard.

2- The second, a fuller and more comprehensive book called: IF? The end of the Messianic lie, by Uriel ben-Mordecai.

Isaiah 49:6

> *He (God) said: it is not enough that you be a servant for Me[66]*
> *alone to raise up the tribes of Jacob and restore the ruins of*
> *Israel, I will also make you a light for the nations, so that My*
> *salvation may reach to the ends of the earth.*

Yeshua is the righteous branch that emerged from Jesse *(Isaiah 11:1, 10, Ruth 4:22)*, the heir to the throne of David, the one worthy to sit at the right hand of God.

Yeshua was obedient to God's will in everything, even to death at the stake, paying the price of the sins of humanity.[67] *(Luke 22:37, 42, Philippians 2:8, 1Peter 3:18, 1Corinthians 15:20-28, Revelation 5:9-10, Isaiah 53)*

Matthew 1:21 states: that this son born, "he will save His people from their sins," this portion of the verse is not quoted from Isaiah 7. Again, the sign is the son, the scion, the heir to the throne of David, here in context of Matthew it is Yeshua, in which this son's birth triggered a specific upcoming event: "he will save His people from their sins."

Only the Messiah, the anointed one of God, the righteous heir to the throne, the one that will do justice and righteousness according to God's will, is the only one that could save His people from their sin's.

This son, this scion, Messiah Yeshua had complete trust and relied solely upon HASHEM, his God. *(John 20:17)*

---

66 "Servant for God" - this verse is a messianic passage referring to the Messiah. i.e. Yeshua the Messiah, the anointed one of God, is the servant of HASHEM, God.

(Hence - Yeshua is not God, but rather he is the servant of God).

67 In no way does remission of sins, gives us a license to sin. But rather, because of gratitude for our salvation, we are a changed people, and begin a new way of walking, a renewed relationship with God and His anointed one.

Yeshua (God's salvation) is the righteous son and king that God brought forth to fulfill the promise made to His servant David. Yeshua is the good shepherd that will restore that which was lost (in the Garden of Eden), by doing justice and righteousness, he is the righteous son worthy to rule God's kingdom.

Luke 1:32-33

> *He will be great/mighty and called son of the Most High*[68], *and HASHEM, God, will give him (Yeshua) the throne of David his (fore-) father,* (through *"Joseph of the house of David"* as identified in Luke 1:27)*; and he (Yeshua) will rule the house of Jacob forever/eternity, there will be no end to his kingdom.*

Revelation 22:16

> *I, Yeshua, have sent my messenger/angel to give you this testimony for the assembly (called out ones): "I am the root and offspring of David, the bright morning star."*

Why does traditional Christianity persist in a pagan belief that Jesus is God, God in the flesh?
Why won't traditional Christians believe Yeshua when he flat out states: that he is David's descendant?

---

68 Son of *Ha'elyon: Son of Most High/Son* of God. To be called a son of God refers to a Tzaddik "a righteous one." Traditional Christianity claims that Yeshua is not only: son of God, but they blatantly and falsely flip Scripture context to refer to: Yeshua as being: God the son.

Yet unbeknownst to traditional Christianity, the children of Israel were considered "son's and daughters of God." Yet no one in their right mind would consider the children of Israel as: God the son/s or God the daughter/s. So why does traditional Christianity spin Scripture "son of God" to somehow mean: "God the son" when applying it to Yeshua? Absurd!

Can the Creator, become the created? Can God the Creator, be a descendant of David, the created?

That which Creates, is now the created; is preposterous!

Chapter Seven

<u>Gabriel Sent by God</u>

Luke 1:26-27
>*26- Now in the sixth month the angel/messenger Gabriel was sent by God to a city in the Galilee/Galil called Nazareth/Natzeret*
>*27- to a virgin <u>to become betrothed/engaged</u> to a man named Joseph/Yosef from the house of David; the virgin's name was Mary/Miryam.*

Before beginning our study on the above verses, just a quick reminder that the Hebrew word for the English word "virgin" in Luke 1:27 is "Betulah - בְּתוּלָה" - the Greek word is "Parthenos - παρθένος," as earlier discussed in a previous chapter that no doubt Mary was a virgin pre-Joseph, and that the Greek word "parthenos" has multiply meanings, whereas the Hebrew is definitive.

Luke chapter one is "pre"- Joseph and Mary's consummation of their marriage.

The English word "betrothed" is taken from the Greek word ἐμνηστευμένην - emnesteumenen (root - μνηστεύω- mnesteuo).

It is defined as:
"to woo, to seek in marriage, to become betrothed, to be betrothed."

In context of verse 27, it is unclear if "ἐμνηστευμένην - emnesteumenen" is in the past, present or future tense, and therefore can only be understood in context with Luke 1:34.

Luke 1:34
> *Now Mary said to the angel/messenger how is this to be (future tense), since I am unaware/do not know (present tense) of a husband/man?*

Had Mary actually been betrothed to Joseph in verse 27, then verse 34 clearly establishes that Mary was unaware of her own betrothal. Therefore, I have translated Luke 1:27 as: "to become betrothed" to reflect that of Mary's own knowledge of her not being aware of her own betrothal.

Let us now turn to the words "not know" in Luke 1:34, it is the exact same word and exact same context as Matthew 1:25.

Matthew 1:25
> *Joseph "did not understand / perceive / recognize / discern" something.*

As already discussed in an earlier chapter, these words do not in anyway infer any type of sexual connotations.

So here in context when Mary states that she "is unaware or does not know" a husband/man, she is simply stating that she is unmarried at this time.

The Greek word ἄνδρα - andra (root - ἀνήρ - aner) is defined as: "man, husband."

Greek makes no distinction between "man and husband."

It's all about context, so in context with Luke 1:34 Mary is simply stating: How can this happen (conceive and bring forth a son Luke 1:31) when she is an unmarried woman.
If one thinks about it both words in context are saying the exact same thing. Mary being a virgin, never having sexual relations with any man, it stands to reason, given her cultural background, that she is unmarried!

Fast forward to our modern day where promiscuity is rampant, one would not conclude in our modern day and culture that being unmarried has any reflection to one's virginity.
But in Biblical times, and being a religious Jew, sexual relations and marriage went hand in hand for both men and women. They would have been ostracized from the community if not stoned to death for sexual cohabitation outside of marriage!

So, when Mary replies to the angel's message to her: "How will this happen/occur, since I do not know (having no knowledge) of a husband," her focus is first and foremost all about first "getting married," certainly not that of acquiring a man in order to get pregnant outside of marriage!
Jewish women of that day not only depended upon either her father or her husband, but it was a matter of structure within their society. Jewish women looked forward to playing their role in their society, it was a great honor and a blessing from God to be married and bear children. (Proverbs 31)

Mary was simply inquiring of the angel of the LORD, how can all of this come about when she is unmarried. Mary's concern is not about getting pregnant out of wedlock, for she fully knows this goes against the very grain of God's Torah. Mary's inquiry is about her desire to be married, the very thing that every Jewish woman of her day desired, which would ultimately lead to having and raising children, fulfilling the Torah, a great blessing.

Deuteronomy 23:18
> *There is not to be promiscuous females among the daughters of Israel, nor is there to be promiscuous males among the sons of Israel.*

The purpose of marriage from a Biblical perspective is companionship and procreation: "It is not good that man be alone; I will make him a helper corresponding to him, man shall cleave to his wife, and they shall become one flesh: *(Gen. 2:18, 24)."*
"Be fruitful, and multiply, and replenish the earth" *(Genesis 1:28)*

Fruitfulness within the confines of marriage is a great blessing and childlessness considered a tragedy and a disgrace. *(Genesis 17:15-17; 30:1-23; Psalms 127: 3; 128)*

Genesis 30:22-23
> *God remembered Rachel; God hearkened to her and He opened her womb. She conceived and bore a son, and said, "God has taken away my disgrace."*

Luke 1:25
> *"The LORD has done this for me (Elizabeth); he has shown me favor at this time, so as to remove my public disgrace."*

It being considered a disgrace to not have children within a marriage, how much more so would it be considered a disgrace in their society of bearing children outside the realm of marriage?

From Luke 1:34 it is clear that Mary was unaware of her own betrothal, therefore Luke 1:27 would most likely be in the future tense "to become betrothed."
However, there is additional information that could be considered into the story line, but it won't change the past, present or future tense of verse 27 along side verse 34.
The fact remains that the conversation was solely with the Angel and Mary, at that time and according to Mary's own words *"I am unaware/do not know (present tense) of a husband/man"* she being unaware of her own betrothal.

Hebraically speaking, it is quite possible that Mary's father had of late procured a husband for her (promised her in marriage), or was in the process of procuring a husband for her; a traditional and widely accepted custom of its day, the father was responsible for their daughter's hand in marriage. Of course the daughter had a say in the matchmaking, she could agree or disagree, generally speaking she would agree as she relied upon her father's wisdom.

As can be seen in the story of Genesis chapter 24, where Abraham had sent his trusted servant Eliezer/Eli'ezer to procure a wife for his son Isaac, in which, Eliezer, according to Abraham's instructions, and his earnest prayer for God's favor in revealing to him a wife for Isaac. After which, Eliezer then went to Rebecca's house to speak with her father, in this particular case it was Rebecca's brother Laban.
The two men discussed the terms and then the terms of that agreement commenced, Eliezer gave Laban what is known as "the bride price."
At this juncture, Scripture does not indicate Rebecca's wishes between the men's agreement and the bride price, we can only

assume she had agreed, because of what had taken place the following morning when Eliezer was ready to return to his master Abraham. Rebecca's brother and mother requested from Eliezer to let Rebecca stay for one year or (at least) ten months then she would go with him. Eliezer bid them to not delay him since God had made his journey successful. The family then called for Rebecca, so as to inquire of her decision if she at this time will go with Eliezer, of which she readily agreed.

Rebecca had accepted without ever having seen her betrothed Isaac. Now on the other end of that same spectrum, Isaac did not know that a wife had been procured for him, and was unfamiliar with the knowledge of being betrothed at this hour and therefore, if an angel had come to him and said that he would be the father of the future king of Israel, Isaac may very well have said to the messenger/angel how is this to be (future tense), since I am unaware/do not know (present tense) of a wife/woman, he being unaware of his own betrothal.

Isaac's inquiry, just like Mary's, would have been focused on "getting married," certainly not impregnating a woman outside of marriage!

Neither Isaac, nor Rebecca had known each other formerly, their betrothal was all pre-arranged by the father's, or by those considered head of household.

So Luke 1:26 and 27 is a prologue; Luke was merely setting the stage for the story to begin unfolding.

When the angel Gabriel visited Mary, the facts are that Mary was a virgin (pre-Joseph), and that Mary herself was unaware of her own betrothal.

Either way "To become betrothed, or/ is betrothed" Mary is factually unaware of her own engagement at the hour of Gabriel's visitation, and Mary's only concern with the message given her, was about "getting married," that is why she inquired "how will (pregnancy) happen/occur when I don't have a husband," not that of "I'm getting pregnant outside of marriage yippy!" Mary was fully aware that children outside of marriage, is taboo.

Luke 1:28-31

> *28- Approaching her (the angel) said, rejoice, favored one, the LORD is with you.*
> *29- Now she was bewildered by his words and considered what kind of greeting this was.*
> *30- So the angel/messenger said to her do not be afraid Mary, for you have found favor with God.*
> *31- Behold, "You will conceive (future tense) in your womb and give birth (future tense) to a son, and you are to call (future tense) his name Yeshua."*

The text only states that sometime in the future Mary will conceive, the text does not state nor imply that God is going to impregnate her.

Many events can and will occur from the present tense of when the message was given to Mary, to the future tense when Mary would conceive. Namely, that Mary will become betrothed to Joseph, then a consummation of that marriage, followed by conception, etc. The natural order by which, God Himself ordained.

Son of God

Luke 1:32

> *He will be great/mighty and called (future tense) son of the Most High, and HASHEM, God, will give (future tense) him (Yeshua) the throne of David his (fore-) father,*

What does it mean to be called "son of the Most High?" Son of the Most High is also the same as saying "son of God."

In Hellenistic thought the term son (υἱός - huios) refers to physical descent. In Hebraic thought the term for son (בֵּן - ben) is very different. "Ben" not only designates physical descent and relationship, but it also refers to younger companions, pupils and members of a group, or a "Particular Characteristic." Most importantly it means one who belongs to God because of one's righteousness. The angels, as members of the heavenly court are called "sons of God." Israel is called the "first-born son of God." *(Exodus 4:22)* The relationship of God and king is like that of father and son. *(2 Samuel 7:12-14)* In Hebraic thought a son was a righteous individual. Messiah was not God's offspring in the sense of a physical child: Yeshua is a son of God because of his righteousness. Yeshua is a "Tzaddik" (Righteous one). Yeshua was anointed by God to lead the people to righteousness so that they could be sons and daughters of God. As a son of God, Messiah Yeshua glorified the Father by turning the people's hearts to God. Matthew identified Yeshua as the son of God. When Yeshua asked his disciples who do you say I am? Peter replied, "you are the Messiah, the son of the living God." *(Matthew 16:16)* [69]

---

69 http://www.torahofmessiah.com of which I highly recommend this website

Luke 1:32

> *The LORD God will give him the throne of David his (fore-) father*

The LORD God will give His anointed one (the Messiah) the throne of his (fore-) father David; Messiah Yeshua is a physical descendant of David the king, of the tribe of Judah.

Yeshua is called "son of God" because of his righteousness. This Father-son language serves to emphasize the special relationship that exists between HASHEM God and Messiah Yeshua.
The fact is, the term "son of God" is always used in an anthropomorphic sense to refer to HASHEM's representative/s. Of course, as the greatest, most obedient, and most exalted of all of HASHEM, God, representative's, Yeshua is, indeed, the "son of God." [70]

Luke 1:33

> *and he (Yeshua) will rule (future tense) the house of Jacob forever/eternity, there will be no end to his kingdom.*

"There will be no end to his kingdom" refers to ruling not only the house of Jacob (the twelve tribes of Israel), but also, all the nations.

HASHEM God will place everything under Messiah Yeshua's feet.

---

[70] http://torahofmessiah.org/?s=son+of+god

David is the speaker here:

Psalms 110:1,

> *HASHEM (יְהֹוָה)[71] said to my Lord/master (אֲדֹנִי)[72]; sit at My right hand, until I make your enemies your footstool.*

Additional supporting Scripture:

Isaiah 49:5-6

> *And now HASHEM, Who formed me from the womb to be a servant to Him, said return Jacob to Him, so that Israel would be gathered to Him; so I was honored in God's eyes and my God was my strength.*
>
> *He (God) said: it is not enough that you be a servant for Me alone to raise up the tribes of Jacob and restore the ruins of Israel, I will also make you a light for the nations, so that My salvation may reach to the ends of the earth.*

---

71 HASHEM - literally THE NAME: "יהוה - YHVH" the ineffable name of God. English Bibles written as: THE LORD, or Jehovah, or ADONAI, or HASHEM.

72 אֲדֹנִי - Adonee. (Not אֲדֹנָי - ADONAI, note the different vowel points. Also note the context of this verse, HASHEM would not be saying to Himself to sit at His right hand). The root is אָדוֹן or אָדֹן - Adon. Adon is a title; Mr., sir, commander, ruler, possessor, proprietor, owner, master, lord.

Here David states that: HASHEM יהוה said to David's master/ Lord אֲדֹנִי adonee (the Messiah): to sit at His right hand, i.e. God has given authority to David's master/Lord, David's descendant Yeshua the Messiah (the anointed one of God).

There is a difference between: LORD, Lord and lord. A few examples, see: *Genesis 18:12*, where Sarah calls Abraham her lord. *Genesis 23:6*, where the children of Heth called Abraham their lord. *Numbers 11:28*, Joshua called Moses my lord. *2Samuel 4:8*, David was called my lord the king. *1Kings 18:7*, Elijah was called my lord.

Psalms 45:8[73]

> *You love righteousness and hate wickedness; therefore has God, your God, anointed you with oil of joy from among your peers.*

Come Over / Overshadow

Luke 1:34-35

> *Now Mary said to the angel/messenger how is this to be (future tense), since I am unaware/do not know (present tense) of a husband? (Mary is unaware of her being betrothed).*
> *The angel/messenger replied and said to her, the Holy Spirit will come (future tense) over you and the power of the Most High will overshadow (future tense) you. And thereby bring forth the consecrated one called (future tense), son of God. (Isaiah 49:1-6; 11:1-2; 11:10; Romans 15:12)*

What exactly does it mean to "come over someone?" Or, as the case may be where most English translators have chosen to translate verse 35 to read: "come upon you." Where again conjecture has led some unsuspecting readers to assume that the Holy Spirit will literally come upon Mary impregnating her. However, that interpretation is far removed from its original intent.

---

73 Hebrew Bible is verse 8, whereas, the Christian Bible is verse 7.

<u>Luke 1:35</u>
και αποκριθεις ο αγγελος ειπεν αυτη πνευμα αγιον
"**επελευσεται   επι**" σε και δυναμις υψιστου
"**επισκιασει**" σοι διο και το γεννωμενον αγιον
κληθησεται υιος θεου

The Greek word in context is in the future tense: ἐπελεύσεται - epeleusetai, of which the root word is: - ἐπέρχομαι (ἐπί, ἔρχομαι) eperchomai (epi, erchomai).

> Of which the Greek definition is:
> to come, to be at hand, to arrive at,
> to go, to come back, to return.

ἐπὶ - epi,
> Of which the Greek definition is:
> over, on, at the time of, at, to.

Therein:

Luke 1:35
> *The Holy Spirit will come over you.*

Starting with the second Greek word, I have chosen to translate the word "over" versus "to," because in context of the words being spoken, the Holy Spirit is doing something more than just arriving.

At some future point in time, God's Spirit will be present over Mary for a purpose, namely that of enabling her to conceive in order to bring forth the consecrated one called son of God (a righteous one). Just as Sarah, Rachel and Elizabeth's barrenness was ended by God's direct involvement, so too, God's direct involvement in "opening the womb" of Mary in order to receive Joseph's seed, so as to bring forth the consecrated one, Messiah Yeshua, humanities salvation.

God opened Elizabeth's womb, of whom was born the one called John the Immerser/Baptist, the one that God had preordained for the very purpose of going ahead of and prepare the way prior to Yeshua's arrival.
(*Luke 1*)

Had God not opened the womb of Sarah, it would not have been possible for Yeshua to be born, as Sarah is Yeshua's (fore-) mother.
No one would accuse Sarah or Elizabeth, when God "opened their womb" to that of God impregnating them without the means of their collective spouses. So too, it is unnecessary for anyone to assume that God's opening of Mary's womb to mean impregnation without Joseph.
God is blessing the fruit of Mary's womb, just as God had blessed the fruit of Sarah and Elizabeth's womb. However, Mary being favored among women, it was she that would give birth to the long awaited arrival of the Messiah, the anointed one of God, the very goal of God's purpose, a means of salvation to the world.

The fact that Mary was "favored among women," it was clearly understood within Judaism that the Messiah would be human, born within that faith, a descendant of David the king of the tribe of Judah.
Any Jewish woman, regardless of her tribal affiliation, was married to a descendant of David the king, through Solomon, et al, knew that they were a possible candidate to giving birth to the Messiah.
Here, we know that Mary was the favored one among women to be the mother of the Messiah, and that God had

orchestrated her marriage to Joseph, a righteous man *(Matthew 1:19)*, and a descendant of David as seen in Matthew chapter one.

Also, I have chosen to translate the word as "over" versus "upon" you, because of an additional Greek word used in that same verse: our third highlighted Greek word is also in the future tense: ἐπισκιάσει˚ - episkiasei. of which the root word is - ἐπισκιάζω - (ἐπι, σκια) episkiazo (epi, skia)

Of which the Greek definition is:
to overshadow, to hide.

Hence: (epi - "**over**," skia - "**shadow**.") So in context, the Greek word ἐπὶ - epi would most probable be translated here as; "over." Therefore (epi, skia) being a compound word would be translated as: "over-shadow" and not that of the word most English translators initially chose for our second word "ἐπὶ - epi:" "upon," otherwise staying true to their text, the word would read: "upon-shadow" a nonsensical word.

It may appear as though I'm being far too tenacious than necessary in regards to the word "over" or "upon." However, there are some readers of the various English Bible translations that have literally assumed based solely on the word "upon" to literally refer to God impregnating Mary without Joseph. They claim that at that moment, when God came "upon" Mary, His coming "upon" her somehow implied "impregnating" her, as if the word "upon" was some type of a mystery code word. Again, that interpretation is far removed from its original intent.

Luke 1:35

The Holy Spirit will come (future tense) "over" you (ensuring conception) and the power of Most High will "overshadow" (future tense) you (protection, in order to bring forth His anointed one, Messiah Yeshua)

In context with:

Matthew 1:18½
> *"in womb/in conception to have/having of the Holy Spirit. (Blessing the fruit of her womb - the power, the will of God ensuring conception and protection, in order to bring forth His anointed one, Messiah Yeshua).*

God opened Mary's womb, enabling her to conceive, just as God had "opened the womb" of Sarah, Rachel and Elizabeth in order for them to receive the seed of their collective husbands. There is no reason to think that God impregnated Mary outside of the seed of Joseph, her husband. For one to claim that God impregnated Mary without Joseph, would certainly banish Yeshua from being a descendant of David his (fore) father, after all, is God a descendant of David? Can the Creator become the created? Absurd!

Yeshua himself states that he is a physical descendant of David:

Revelation 22:16
> *I, Yeshua, have sent my messenger/angel to give you this testimony for the assembly (called out ones): "I am the root and offspring of David, the bright morning star."*

Yeshua frequently referred to himself as a "son of man," meaning he is a descendant of the human race. Precisely, he is a physical descendant of David the king of the tribe of Judah, a qualifying fact to his candidacy of being the Messiah.

Matthew tells us Yeshua's genealogy, a son through Abraham, Judah, David and Joseph. *(Matthew 1:1-17)*
The angel of the LORD reminded Joseph that he too is a descendant of David *(Matthew 1:20)*, therein qualifying Yeshua as a legal heir to the throne of David.

"The Holy Spirit will come over you and the power of the Most High will overshadow you," is symbolizing the presence and power of God. In this context, to come over and overshadow is the power of God "opening Mary's womb" in order to receive "Joseph's seed" (descendant of David's) at the precise moment in time and the overshadowing, is the presence of God "shielding and protecting" for the purpose of bringing forth "the consecrated one" the Messiah, called the "son of God" a righteous one, one that would lead the people to God, bringing salvation to the world, the intended objective goal.

When the Holy Spirit comes "over" a believer, it is symbolizing the presence and power of God descending and operating in ones life, as can be seen in Act 1:8, "you will receive power when the Holy Spirit comes over you." Certainly no one would accuse a believer that has received the gift of the Holy Spirit as to being impregnated when the Holy Spirit has "come over" them.
Likewise, no one would accuse Moses (Moshe) or the others of being impregnated when they were "overshadowed" at the mount of transfiguration.

Luke 9:34

> *While he was speaking this, a cloud came and overshadowed them, and fear came upon them as they entered the cloud.*

There is no reason to think that God impregnated another mans wife, yet unbeknownst to the traditional

Christian/Messianic mindset, their claim that God having impregnated Mary (another mans wife), is liken to accusing the Holy God of adultery, an act that God Himself considers unholy.

With God, Nothing is Impossible

Luke 1:36-37

> *36- Behold, your relative Elizabeth even she conceived a son in her old age, and this is the sixth month for her who was called barren.*
> *37- For with God, nothing is impossible.*

Mary inquires of the Angel of the LORD: How can all of this take place, since I am unaware/do not know (present tense) of a husband. The Angel of the LORD gives Mary a simple and direct answer: Elisabeth who is beyond the age of reproduction is pregnant, that which is thought to be impossible, God has made possible, is there anything too hard for the LORD!

Mary quickly acknowledged this fact and stated:

Luke 1:38

> *..."I am the servant of the LORD; let it happen to me according to your message," and so the messenger/angel departed from her.*

Paraphrasing Mary's inquiry of the Angel of the LORD: How can I conceive a child when I am without a husband? The Angel of the LORD gives Mary a simple and direct answer: Elisabeth who is beyond the age of reproduction, is in fact pregnant, that which is thought to be impossible, God has made possible, is there anything too hard for the LORD!

The angel of the LORD is not saying to Mary, ah don't worry about a husband you don't need a husband to conceive a child, God will impregnate you and get you married off in time so no one will suspect or accuse you of fooling around prior to marriage. Seriously! Wouldn't that just be a deception? Do you believe that God would do such a thing? Well that's just what traditional Christianity claims God has done with their version of the virgin birth story!

God brought forth the righteous one, Yeshua the Messiah (God's anointed one), because humanity is in need of salvation and restoration. Had God actually impregnated Mary as traditional Christianity insists on claiming, then Yeshua's going to the cross would be of no effect for salvation to the world. Yeshua must be fully human and only human, just as the first human being Adam was, and all humanity is, which leads us to our final chapter of this book.

Chapter Eight

The Garden of Eden
Wisdom - versus - Knowledge

In this final chapter we'll articulate as to why the tree of knowledge of good and evil is in fact a fig tree and not that as supposed by the populist, an apple tree. Additionally, but most importantly, digging deeper into the symbolic meaning of the fig tree and its intended purpose.

Whereas, an apple tree just won't do, masquerading itself as the real deal with nothing to show for itself except cunning deceptions: an invention of the snake/serpent.[74]

---

74 The Hebrew word na'chaysh not only means snake/serpent, but also means to twist, corrupt, or pervert. It is a play on words in Genesis 3:1 (giving depth to the story). Now the na'chaysh (snake - one who twist, perverts) was more crafty (sly/cunning) than any wild animal, which The LORD GOD had made.

John 8:44

> *You belong to your father Satan, wanting to do your fathers desires. From the beginning he was a murderer, and he has never stood by the truth, because there is no truth in him. When he tells a lie, he's speaking in character, because he is a liar and the father of it.*

Beginning with:

Genesis 3:6-8

> *6- And the woman perceived that the tree was good for eating and that it was a delight to the eyes, and that the tree was desirable as a means of wisdom, and she took of its fruit and ate; and she gave also to her husband with her, and he ate.*
> *7- Then the eyes of both of them were opened and they realized that they were naked; and they sewed fig leaves together and made themselves loin covering.*
> *8- They heard the manifestation of the voice of HASHEM God in the evening breeze, and the man and his wife hid from the presence of HASHEM God among the trees in the garden.*

Notice in the above Scripture verses that several actions had occurred back to back:

1- Eve took and ate
2- Eve gave the fruit to Adam, who was standing next to her
3- Adam took and ate
4- Both realized they were naked
5- They sewed fig leaves as loin cloth
6- They heard the voice of the LORD GOD and hid themselves

Notice that in verses 6 and 7 that Adam and Eve had never moved from their position where they were originally standing when they ate of the forbidden fruit, and having clothed themselves with fig leaves. It was only in verse 8 after hearing the voice of the LORD GOD that they had then moved from their position when they went to hide themselves among the trees in the garden.

So it stands to reason that the forbidden fruit was indeed a fig tree since they hadn't moved from their position when they clothed themselves with fig leaves.

So the populist having incorrectly identified the tree of knowledge of good and evil as being an apple tree, and those reading this book may very well say that learning that the tree was in fact a fig tree is but an interesting tidbit.

Oh, but there is more, so much more, lets begin peeling back the layers.

Since the inception of the fall of humankind and the consequence expulsion from the Garden of Eden, humankind has been in need of redemption.

In the Garden of Eden, the word of the snake/serpent prevailed over the Word of God. The allure of the forbidden fruit became irresistible to Eve. What a bitter irony in her seeing that "it was good."

During the creation process, God had repeatedly said that things were good. Now the whole idea of what is good had become debased in the human mind. Good is no longer defined by God's verdict as the Creator, but by the senses and utilitarian values of a human being, the creation.

At that moment, man changes the representation of the tree of knowledge to a twisted and perverted form of knowledge. Good and evil become concepts defined by the senses of men, rather than being dependant on the will of God.

The Tree of Life was in the middle of the garden, in the very center and heart of the garden, just as a human heart is center in the body. The heart distributes life-sustaining blood to the entire body.

This is also true of God's Word, which the Tree of Life represents, with regard to our spiritual body and its nourishment. Proverbs 3:18 states the Torah (God's Word) is a Tree of Life for all those who grasp it.[75]

Salvation / Restoration

Mark 11:1, 12-14, 20-22

> 1- *As they were nearing Jerusalem towards Bethplage/Beit-pagei and Bethany/Beit-anyah by the Mount of Olives, he (Yeshua) sent two of his disciples*
>
> 12- *The next day as they left Bethany, he felt hungry*
> 13- *and seeing in the distance a fig tree in leaf, he went to see if he could find anything on it. When he came up to it, he found nothing but leaves, for it wasn't fig season.*
> 14- *He said to it: "May no one ever eat fruit from you again!" And his disciples heard it.*
>
> 20- *In the morning, as they passed by, they saw the fig tree withered from its roots.*
> 21- *And Peter/Kefa, remembering, said to him, "Rabbi, Look! The fig tree that you cursed has dried up!"*
> 22- *Yeshua responded, saying to them to have faith/trust in God.*

---

75 Nehemiah Restoration Fund

Now keeping in mind that Yeshua is just two days away from going to the cross, as well as, in 2 ¼ days the festival of Passover will begin at sunset.

In Mark 11:1 there are two Biblical towns called Beit-pagei/Bethphage and Beit-anyah/Bethany, Hebrew names are very significant as they lend insight to the narrative. Beit-pagei means "place of the unripe fig," and Beit-anyah means "place of the poor," (possible dual understanding, place of the humble or poor in spirit).

Here we will focus on Beit-pagei the place of the unripe fig. In Mark 11:13, Yeshua spots a fig tree in leaf, but there isn't any fruit on the tree, "for it wasn't fig season."

Now Passover is in the spring, generally our March or April, whereas, fig season is not until June.

Now Yeshua certainly knew all about the various plant seasons as he had often incorporated plant life and its cycles into many of his teaching parables. These verses in Mark are no different, here Yeshua is teaching a great lesson, parable style, first to his disciples and then in turn to every generation thereafter.

In Mark 11:14, Yeshua curses the fig tree: "May no one ever eat/partake fruit from you again!"

It only appears as though Yeshua had cursed the fig tree do to his hunger, as the text does state in Mark 11:12 "He felt hungry," but things aren't always as they appear.

In Mark 11:20-24, the next day Yeshua's disciples take note that the fig tree has withered all the way to its roots. Yeshua utilizes this to teach them to have faith/trust in God.

So here one might think that's the end of the lesson, but again, there is so much more, however his disciples won't fully grasp the impact of this teaching until after Yeshua's resurrection.

Now on the other hand, the apostle Paul, who was not a disciple of Yeshua's until well after Yeshua's resurrection, Paul came to understand this particle parable of Mark 11 with crucial clarity, of which, Paul makes evident in 1Corinthians 15:21-28. Here we will focus on verses 21 and 22.

1Corinthians 15:21-22

> *For since death came through a man (Adam), also the resurrection of the dead has come through a man (Yeshua). For just as in connection with Adam all die, so in connection with the Messiah all will be made alive.*

The first human being Adam/A'dam[76], by disobeying God, not only brought death, but also expulsion from the Garden of Eden (paradise), sin being the element that separates us from God.

Since the fall of humankind in the Garden of Eden, one might inquire as to how restoration of humankind's relationship to God be restored?

Once again, the apostle Paul elaborates:

1 Corinthians 15:45-49

> *45- Therefore, it is written: "the first human-being Adam became a living-being," but the last Adam (human-being Yeshua) became a life-giving Spirit.*
> *46- The first is not spiritual, but the natural (earthly/worldly - 1Corinthians 2:14 afterwards comes the spiritual).*
> *47- The first human-being is of the earth (worldly), made of dust; the second human-being is of Heaven (godly/spiritual).*
> *48- Just as those made of dust, are such (earthly/worldly), also, those of Heaven are such (godly/spiritual).*
> *49- Just as we have borne the image of the man of dust, we also will bear the image of the man of the heavenly.*

---

76 The Hebrew word A'dam literally translated means humankind or human being. A'dam is not Adam's name per se, but rather he is, in this case the first of his kind, a human being.

Romans 5:18
> *In other words, just as it was through one transgression that all humankind came under condemnation, so also it is through one righteous act that all humankind comes to be considered righteous.*

It is in Mark 11, just two days before Yeshua goes to the cross (the righteous one paying the price for humankinds sins), Yeshua curses that through which sin entered the world; a fig tree (Genesis 3:7), symbolic of the tree of knowledge of good and evil, gained apart from God's Torah (God's Word, Wisdom/Instruction) the Tree of Life. In so doing, Yeshua intercepts man's quest to obtain knowledge, first by asserting that knowledge is but the Torah's handmaiden "Proverbs 1:7; the fear of HASHEM is the beginning of knowledge," and second by redirecting our journey to knowledge, only via the Tree of Life, "Proverbs 2:6; For HASHEM gives wisdom; from His mouth comes knowledge and understanding." "Proverbs 3:7; Don't be conceited about your own wisdom; but fear HASHEM, and turn from evil." [77]

Yeshua the Messiah, the anointed one of God, "the consecrated one," called the "son of God" a righteous one, this one would not only pay the price for humankinds sins, but he would lead the people to God, bringing salvation and restoration to the world, the very intended objective goal.

---

77 Nehemiah Restoration Fund

Reinventing the Wheel

Has traditional Christianity reinvented the wheel when it comes to certain belief systems from their interpretation of the English Bible?
Does the traditional Christian belief of the virgin birth really matter, after all it isn't a salvation document, so what difference does it make?

To me, and I hope to you as well that it does make a difference, because if we go throughout our lives embracing half truth's, what will the quality and direction of our life be?
A lie or a half lie is nothing more than robbing a person of their free will, their God given right to choose.
A lie or half lie is a pollution of reality, intended to cause a person to go in the direction the liar desires the person to go in. So who benefits from a lie, the liar or the one lied to?

The question begging to be asked is, who and what lie behind this mask of separation?
It's none other than the anti-messiah, Satan himself! The anti-messiah has minions of followers doing his dastardly dark perversions, masked by a pretense, most that follow aren't even aware they are actually doing his bidding.

What is the anti-messiah, isn't it someone or something that is masquerading as the real Messiah, in order to deceive and destroy? Wasn't Satan right there in the Garden of Eden, nudging, twisting the words to entice Adam and Eve to partake in the forbidden fruit, of which, that disobedience was separation from God.

Revelation 18:4-5

> Then hearing another voice out of heaven say: Come out of her my people, so that you do not take part in her sins lest you receive of her plagues.

For her sins are a sticky mass heaped up to heaven, and God has remembered her iniquities.

Come out of her come out of Babylon.

The first step to leaving Babylon is to recapture the true identity of Yeshua the Messiah as set forth by God Himself. Therein, giving him back to his people intact, by obeying our calling in Romans 11:11-36. Identifying Yeshua as he really is, and then giving him back to the Jewish people, one whom they can recognize, the one whom they seek but can't identify through traditional Christian eyes, so that they may embrace their Yeshua̲h̲ (salvation) as well, that we as a whole joining the commonwealth of Israel as one united people, serving HASHEM, God, under the leadership of King Yeshua, the anointed one of God. Paradise restored!

Anything short of that would be like placing our hope in a pseudo messiah.

A Fresh Look at Scripture

Matthew 1:16, 18-25

> *16- Jacob was the father of Joseph, the husband of Mary, out of it (this union) was born Yeshua, called the Messiah.*

> *18- Now the birth of Yeshua the Messiah happened this way. Betrothed his mother Mary to Joseph, before their coming together (consummating the marriage), he found out/learned (that) in womb/in conception to have/having of the Holy*

Spirit (Blessing the fruit of her womb - the power, the will of God ensuring conception and protection, in order to bring forth His anointed one, Messiah Yeshua).

19- Now Joseph her husband was righteous and not willing to disgrace her, resolved secretly to release/divorce her (from the marriage contract).

20- But while he was considering this (divorce vs.19), an angel of the LORD appeared to him in a dream and said, Behold, "Joseph son of David," do not fear to take Mary your wife (consummate the marriage), because this with her to beget/to father, is of the Holy Spirit (God blessing their union).

21- And (she) will (future tense) bear a son and call his name Yeshua, for he will save His people from their sins.

22- Now all this came about in order to fulfill what the LORD had said through the prophet,

23- Behold "the young woman will (future tense) conceive and bear a son and call his name Immanuel." which is translated "God with us" (God has not abandoned His people).

24- Then Joseph rose up from his sleep to do that what the angel of the LORD commanded him and took his wife (consummated the marriage),

25- but (Joseph) did not understand (something vs.21-23), until she bore their/his son and called his name Yeshua (God's Salvation).

Luke 1:26-38

26- Now in the sixth month the angel/messenger Gabriel was sent by God to a city in the Galilee called Nazareth

27- to a virgin to become betrothed/engaged to a man named Joseph from the house of David; the virgin's name was Mary.

28- Approaching her (the angel) said, rejoice, favored one, the LORD is with you.

29- Now she was bewildered by his words and considered what kind of greeting this was.

30- So the angel/messenger said to her do not be afraid Mary, for you have found favor with God.

31- Behold "You will conceive (future tense) in your womb and give birth (future tense) to a son, and you are to call (future tense) his name Yeshua."

32- He will be great/mighty and called son of the Most High, and HASHEM, God, will give him (Yeshua) the throne of David his (fore-) father, (through *"Joseph of the house of David"* as identified in Luke 1:27);

33- and he (Yeshua) will rule the house of Jacob forever/ eternity, there will be no end to his kingdom.

34- Now Mary said to the angel/messenger how is this to be (future tense), since I am unaware/do not know (present tense) of a husband? (Mary is unaware of her being betrothed).

35- The angel/messenger replied and said to her, the Holy Spirit will come (future tense) over you (blessing the fruit of her womb / ensuring conception) and the power of the Most High will overshadow (future tense) you (protection). And thereby bring forth the consecrated one called (future tense), son of God.

36- Behold, your relative Elizabeth even she conceived a son in her old age, and this is the sixth month for her who was called barren.

37- For with God, nothing is impossible.

38- Then Mary said, "I am the servant of the LORD; let it happen to me according to your message," and so the messenger/angel departed from her.

Its time to wake up, "come out of Babylon" (confusion) and its "mystery religion," and come to the Promised Land, up to Jerusalem, where God has chosen to place His Name.

Jeremiah 16:19-20

> *HASHEM, my strength, my stronghold and my refuge on the day of tribulation! The nations will come to You from the ends of the earth, saying, "Our ancestors inherited nothing but lies, futile idols, completely useless.*
> *Can a person make gods for himself? – They are not gods!"*

Isaiah 2:3[78]

> *Many peoples will go and say, "Come let us go up to the mountain of HASHEM, to the house of the God of Jacob, He will teach us of His ways and we will walk in His paths." For out of Tzion/Zion will go forth Torah, the word of HASHEM from Jerusalem.*

---

78 Micah 4:2

Notes

Notes

Notes

Notes

Notes

Notes

www.ingramcontent.com/pod-product-compliance
Lightning Source LLC
Chambersburg PA
CBHW070957040426
42443CB00007B/550